2 O 1 2

THE MEANING AND

THE MESSAGE

2 0 1 2
THE MEANING AND THE MESSAGE

BOB WAXMAN

Paragon House
St. Paul, Minnesota

Published in the United States by
Paragon House
1925 Oakcrest Avenue, Suite 7
St. Paul, MN 55113

Cover design by Tobias Norton

Library of Congress Cataloging-in-Publication Data

Waxman, Bob, 1956-
2012 : the meaning and the message / by Bob Waxman.
    p. cm.
    Summary:"The end of the Mayan calendar on December 21, 2012, has
caused many prophecies about major events or the end of the world. Bob
Waxman's concise account of the Mayan culture and calendar provides the
reader with a clear understanding of the facts and fictions surrounding the
2012 phenomenon"—Provided by publisher.
    Includes bibliographical references.
    ISBN 978-1-55778-890-0 (pbk. : alk. paper) 1. Mayan calendar. 2. Two
thousand twelve, A.D. 3. Prophecies. 4.
    Twenty-first century—Forecasts. 5. Social prediction. 6. Maya astrology.
7. Maya philosophy. 8. Mayas—Social life and customs. I. Title. II. Title:
Two thousand twelve. III. Title: Two thousand and twelve. IV. Title: Twenty
twelve.
    F1435.3.C14W39 2010
    972'.01--dc22
                                                            2010011869

The paper used in this publication meets the minimum requirements of
American National Standard for Information Sciences—Permanence of
Paper for Printed Library Materials, ANSIZ39.48-1984.
Manufactured in the United States of America
    10 9 8 7 6 5 4 3 2 1

For current information about all releases from Paragon House,
visit the web site at http://www.ParagonHouse.com

With special thanks to:
Sandy Brown & Sandy Norton

Acknowledgements

I wish to thank and acknowledge: The Center for Positive Living, Sarasota, Florida; Unity Church of Sarasota, Florida; Longboat Key Education Center, Florida; Rav Azriel Abraham (1902-1998) scholar, writer, and educator; Dr. Sheldon Solomon of Skidmore College; Dr. Carol Parrish for her wisdom and friendship; Carol B. Green for her friendship, support, and keen intellect; Transmedia Group for their excellent PR; Irwin, Stella, Richard, Debbie, Nikki, Tammi, Lauren and Michael for their love and support; Rosemary Yokoi of Paragon House for publishing my first book; and Muriel Trachman for her unforgettable inspiration.

Contents

PREFACE

Here's the big question: Why does the Mayan Long Count Calendar end on December 21, 2012, at 11:11 PM (Yucatan time)? Despite what you may have heard, there is only one incomplete historical reference attempting to answer this question. This message from the Mayans can be deciphered as follows: A dramatic planetary change is coming in 2012, and humanity will never be the same again.

First, it is essential to point out that the Mayas had absolutely no intention of predicting an apocalyptic, "end-of-time" scenario for 2012. In fact, when viewed in proper perspective, *the ultimate meaning* of 2012 is an optimistic, uplifting, and hopeful message for humanity.

Archeologists and mythologists believe the Mayas were predicting an age of enlightenment on 13.0.0.0.0 (December 21, 2012). There isn't any scientific evidence to suggest that doomsday will strike. There are, however, plenty of speculations based on Mayan mythology that are inspiring fear-based storylines for Hollywood. A recent film in the *Indiana Jones* series exaggerated a Mayan myth about 13 crystal skulls that must come together to save the world from certain destruction. According to the storyline, if the 13 skulls do not reunite, Earth will be knocked off its axis and saunter off into outer space. While this type of screenplay makes for an exciting movie, there are absolutely no predictions from the Mayas that foretell of such an event occurring in 2012. This type of sensationalism only creates fear and confusion and conjures up images of New York City being decimated, along with the usual decapitation of the Statue of Liberty.

Unfortunately, by distorting the ultimate meaning of 2012, the truth of the Mayan message takes second place to the entertainment industry's fear-based strategy of selling movie tickets. This version is filled with death and destruction and countless theories of planetary annihilation. Consequently, the 2012 doomsayers are anxiously waiting to point out every space-based threat imaginable. These include "Planet X" smashing into Earth, thousands of meteorite impacts, comets blasting through the atmosphere, black holes interfering with Earth's gravity, killer solar flares, gamma ray bursts, a new ice age, pole reversals, and magnetic shifts.

Fortunately, there is no evidence whatsoever that any of these disasters will occur in 2012. However, it is amazing how misdirected speculations have generated such an avalanche of publicity and fear-mongering.

From a scientific standpoint, the Mayan Long Count Calendar is specifically designed to mark the conclusion of a time cycle. The Calendar's ending in 2012 is simply a line of demarcation between two cosmic ages. The ancient Mayas were not trying to scare future generations, but rather, they were foretelling the coming of enlightenment in the next era. According to Mayan Priest Don Alejandro Cirilo Oxla, the prophecy for the next cycle reveals the following:

> Let the dawn come. Let all the people and all the creatures have peace, let all things live happily, for the love must not only be between humans, but between all living things. They said, "We are the children of the Sun, we are the children of time, and we are the travelers in space. May all the songs awaken, may all the dancers awaken. May all the people and all things live in peace, for you are the valleys, you are the mountains, you are the trees, you are the very air you breathe."
>
> Now is the time of return of the grandmothers and grandfathers. Now is the time of the return of the elders. Now is the time of the return of the wise ones.
>
> And the wise ones are all of you.
>
> Now is the time to go out into the world and spread the light. The sacred flame has been kept for this purpose and now the time approaches when you will be required to love all things,

to love a world that has gone crazy, to rebalance the heavens and the Earth. For the Time of Warning has come to pass and the Warriors of the Rainbow are now beginning to be born, The Vale of Tears, the Nine Hells, is over and it is time to prepare for the 13 Heavens. The ancestors are returning, my brothers and sisters, and we do not have long. Now is the time that the prophecies will be fulfilled.

Mayan scholars believe the Long Count Calendar will simply continue "rolling over" (like an odometer) after reaching December 21, 2012 (13.0.0.0.0). It will reset once again on December 21, 7125 (20.0.0.0.0); however, we need not worry about that transition right now. Meanwhile, the time of "12 Baktun and 13 Ahau" is fast approaching, and according to *the ultimate meaning of 2012*, an old world is dying, while a new one is being born.

INTRODUCTION

If you are reading this book before December 21, 2012, you may be worried or anxious about all the doomsday prophecies being credited to the Quiche Mayas. Please relax and rest assured that the Mayas never had any intention of predicting a catastrophic global event for 2012. Despite the barrage of hype on TV and the internet, reports of the Earth's demise "have been greatly exaggerated."

So, here's the boring truth of the matter: there are no Mayan prophecies that predict the end of the world in 2012. In fact, the Mayas didn't even foresee their own demise in 910 CE. Therefore, it is highly unlikely that they could predict the arrival of a worldwide flood in 2012. So here's the good news: You don't need to build an Ark, invest in a fall-out shelter, or move to a mountain top.

Now, the question is: where do these dire prophecies come from? Believe it or not, they come from the wild imaginations of contemporary writers who are trying to convince the public that a single drawing in a Mayan text (*The Dresden Codex*) is signaling the end of times. In this illustration, we see the Mayan goddess Ix-Chel pouring a jar of water onto a Lord of the Underworld with an inscription reading, "black sky", "black earth".

However, let's hold on a minute—one thing missing—there's no *date* associated with this depiction and no reference whatsoever to 2012! Therefore, we have no reason to believe that this drawing symbolizes an oncoming flood in 2012 (13.0.0.0.0). Alternatively, many scholars believe that this drawing is connected to the most important time of the Mayan year—the rainy season. Without heavy rains, the Mayas could not grow sufficient amounts of corn to sustain themselves. So, it is safe to say that the Mayas were much more concerned about the arrival of the next rainy season than with the arrival of 2012.

Unfortunately for the *2012* film-makers, we cannot give the Mayas credit for predicting an apocalypse. There is an overwhelming lack of evidence for proposing such an idea. The simple fact is that very few Mayan texts are still in existence, and therefore, trying to find prophecies regarding a forthcoming disaster in 2012 is a fruitless endeavor. Meanwhile, in the surviving texts, there is not a word of caution about the day the Mayan Calendar ends in 2012. However, the Long Count Calendar still has great significance and exemplifies the Mayan genius for accurately measuring the beginning and ending of "an astronomical age."

Remarkably, the Mayas understood the complexities of calculating long periods of time, and their 13 baktun cycle (the Long Count Calendar) measures one complete period of 25,625 years.

Most researchers agree that the Mayan time cycles were based on planetary and galactic patterns that could be seen with the naked eye. They understood the Sun's relationship with the Earth and could predict the precise time of the equinoxes and solstices. They also understood the Sun's position in the Milky Way and discovered methods for measuring its circular path according to the position of the stars. The Mayas were obsessed with this form of astronomical time-keeping, and their calendars have proven to be incredibly accurate. They had a deep understanding of lunar, solar, and planetary cycles that allowed them to predict the coming of a solar eclipse—even thousands of years into the future.

The Mayas could be called "shamanic scientists" because they were fully aware of the benefits of living in natural time. They knew that our life in the Universe is part of a much larger cycle of time. Similarly, other great civilizations invented advanced systems for measuring grand cycles of cosmic time. For example, the Hopi of North America believe in time periods that involve the creation and destruction of former world ages. They continue to mark the end of "a cyclical world" upon the appearance of Saquasohuh or the Blue Star Spirit. According to legend, the Blue Star Spirit is responsible for ending the old age and planting new seeds for bringing forth the next one. The Mayas have a similar legend and believe that Kukulcan (or Quetzalcoatl) will return to the world one day and save humanity. Upon the arrival of this savior god, the New Age begins, and life becomes a "Heaven on Earth" forevermore (sound familiar?).

Also—there is a "time designation issue" that needs to be addressed. The confusion surrounds the Mayan numerical sequences of "Worlds" and "Suns." Most authors favor the designation of an up-coming *Fifth World* and *Sixth Sun* to represent the upcoming age, however, the Mayan Elders prefer to call the next cycle - the *Fifth World* and *Fifth Sun*. For our purposes, we are choosing to rely on the accuracy of the Mayan Elders, and will use the terms: Fifth World and Fifth Sun when referring to the next time-period of 2012 and beyond. Therefore, the current Fourth Age began on August 11, 3114 BCE, and will end on December 21, 2012 CE.

○—————————○

Now, let's take a closer look at the Mayan people and discover who they were, what they accomplished, and what they left behind.

Chapter 1

EARLY MESOAMERICAN CULTURES

We need to clearly establish the origins of the Mayas. There is evidence that tribes migrating across Asia did not go directly to Mexico to begin the Mayan culture. There were many steps along the way. One theory posits that a large population of hunters and gatherers moved across the Bering Strait into the area that is now Alaska. It is presumed that others continued the journey and headed south and east.

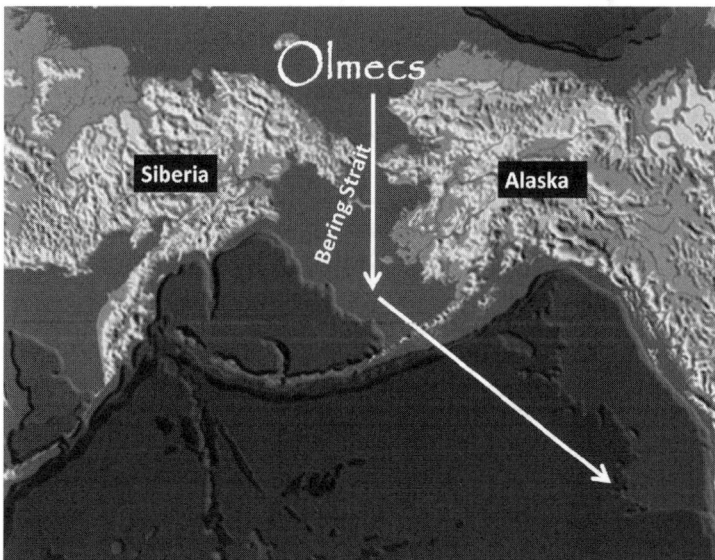

Early predecessors of the Mayans may have traveled across the Bering Strait into what is now Alaska

According to most anthropologists, these nomads settled in Canada and North America and left their footprints in the form of ceremonial and burial mounds. These people formed tribes whose members became hunters, planters, and harvesters. They built villages in the cooler climate of the North during the summer, and in winter, moved south for warmth and to find food. Following the migration of animals, they hunted, harvested crops, and planted corn to feed their people.

Continuing on their journey south, the nomads settled in areas that are now Belize, Guatemala, Honduras, El Salvador, and Mexico. These tribes settled in lush areas where their crops flourished, and a society of independent villages emerged. With their remarkable talents, they left behind a legacy and culture that continues to fascinate modern scholars and archeologists.

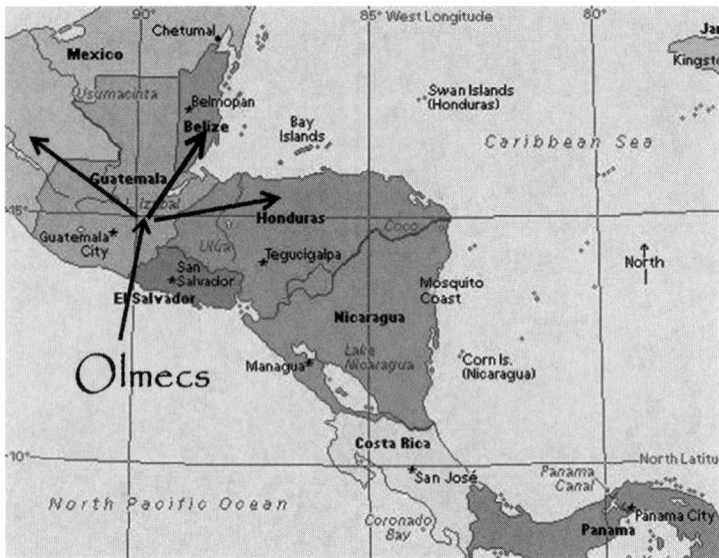

The Olmecs settled in the areas known today as
Guatemala, Honduras, and El Salvador

It should be noted that there is also evidence, including accounts recorded in a Mayan text called the *Popol Vuh*, that indicate that the Mayans came from the East, across the sea. We will look into this further as we explore the *Popol Vuh* and theories of trans-Atlantic migration in later chapters of this book.

BEFORE THE MAYAS

Over time, the first Mesoamerican civilizations began to emerge. One of the most influential were the Olmecs (2000 BCE-400 BCE), an ancient Pre-Columbian people who lived in a region known as the Olmec Heartland. These are areas of South Central Mexico, along the lowlands of the Gulf of Mexico, in the modern-day states of Veracruz and Tabasco. This area is considered to be the birthplace of the Olmec culture. The land was swampy with small hills, and inactive volcanoes dotted the landscape. In this fertile area, the Olmec civilization flourished, and city-temple complexes were built in San Lorenzo, Tenochtitlan, La Venta, Tres Zapotes, and Laguna de los Cerros. They used waterways for transportation which were comparable to the Egyptian use of the Nile River. This was a highly productive agricultural environment, which allowed the development of a dense population to congregate in one area.

Olmec means "rubber people" in the native Aztec language of Nahuatl. The term refers to the ancient Olmec practice of extracting latex from local rubber trees. They would then mix the juice from a "rubber tree vine" with Ipomoea Alba into a mixture to create rubber. This practice is thought to have begun in approximately 1600 BCE and is supported by the discovery of a dozen rubber balls dating back to this period. A rubber ball court, used by the Olmecs to play a ball game, was found in an Olmec sacrificial site located six miles east of the San Lorenzo area of Tenochtitlan in Veracruz. Until a few years ago, it was obscured by dense overgrowth and is now considered the earliest ball court in Central America. We will look at ball courts in more detail in Chapter 4.

Over time, an elite class began to emerge in San Lorenzo who

Olmec stone carving of ball player

wanted to acquire artistic sculptures with religious symbols. These luxurious artifacts of jade and obsidian had to be imported from the far reaches of Guatemala. Therefore, to obtain these treasures, the Olmecs had to create an extensive trade route throughout the modern area of Latin America. Likewise, Olmec art was purchased by this elite class, as well as by non-Olmec chieftains who strengthened their political status by owning these beautiful items. Because of these extensive merchant trade routes, the influence of Olmec art and culture spread throughout the region and beyond. This explains why wide assortments of artifacts, figurines, monuments, and icons have been discovered at archeological sites located hundreds of miles from the original Olmec region. Additionally, Olmec influences have been found in Mexico, Morelos, Guerrero, and in cave paintings that feature Olmec iconography.

Later on in the 900s BCE, San Lorenzo was abandoned due to drought conditions and famine, and La Venta became the most important Olmec center until 400 BCE. Within the city were phenomenal displays of power and wealth, including the Great

Pyramid of La Venta, which was the largest Mesoamerican structure at the time. Although the Pyramid has been eroding for 2500 years, it still stands 112 feet high above the flat landscape. Within the storehouses of this Great Pyramid, archeologists have found artistic figurines, mosaics, polished jade, pottery, and other objects of art.

For reasons that are unclear, the Olmec civilization seems to have disappeared sometime between 400–350 BCE. Historians are unable to explain why this thriving culture vanished so suddenly, but the limited information available has led to theories that the population disappeared as the result of serious environmental issues. Perhaps unfavorable farming conditions caused by drought or extreme volcanic activity were responsible for the disappearance or relocation of the Olmec people.

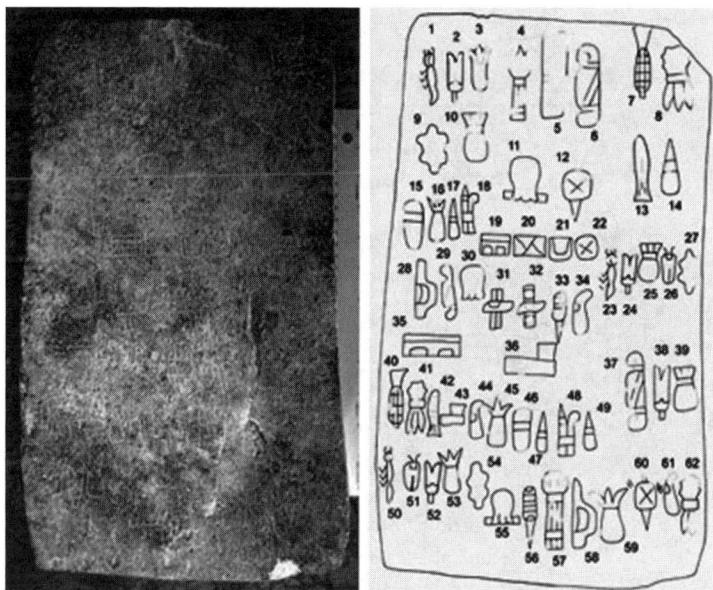

Cascajal Block, the earliest known writing in the Americas.
This illustration demonstrates 62 symbols.

First Mesoamerican Writing

The Olmecs probably developed the first writing system in the Western Hemisphere. Archeologists claim that test samples from this period trace back to 900 BCE-650 BCE. These dates precede the oldest known writing system of the Zapotecs in Oaxaca and Chiapas. At the Olmec San Andres dig site in 2002, artifacts were found showing birds, speech scrolls, and glyphs. These symbols are similar to later Mayan hieroglyphs and are known as the Cascajal Block.

Olmec Calendar

Used by so many of the Mesoamerican civilizations, the Long Count Calendar may be another invention of the Olmecs, not the Mayas.

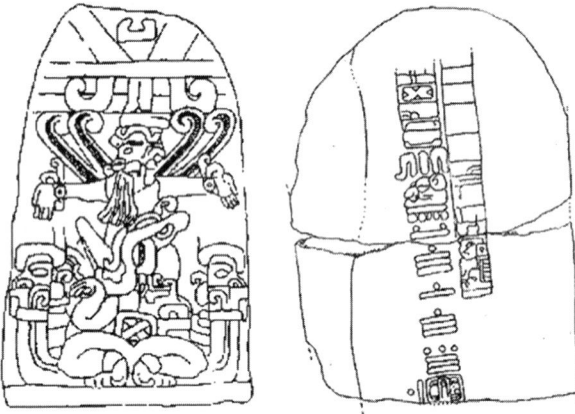

Front   Back

Stela C from Tres Zapotes
This is the second oldest Long Count date yet discovered.
The numerals 7.16.6.16.18 translate to September 3, 32 BCE.
The glyphic images surrounding the date are representative
of a surviving sample of Epi-Olmec script.

This claim is supported by a number of artifacts with markings of early Long Count dates found outside the accepted Mayan region. The Stela C (stone tablet with inscription) from Tres Zapotes, predates the Mayas, and this evidence appears to point to the Long Count Calendar's being invented by the Olmecs. Indeed, three of these six artifacts were found within the Olmec civilization. Conversely, others believe that the Olmecs did not develop the Long Count Calendar because no artifacts have been found prior to the 4th century BCE, when the Olmecs disappeared.

HISTORICAL TIME PERIODS OF THE MAYAS

The Mayas, who some historians believe to be descended from the Olmecs, represent one of the most fascinating cultures in world history. Like the Olmecs, they used a comprehensive form of writing and an extensive calendar system. And yet, there is very little recorded documentation about who they were. The information that is known about this ancient civilization is based primarily on the art, pottery, and ruins that have been uncovered by archaeologists and historians over the years.

Most historians believe that the early Mayas were made up of many groups of indigenous people who shared a common religion and used the same calendar system. They also developed a unique writing system which included a set of hieroglyphs that allowed these groups with various dialects to communicate with each other.

Archeologists have divided the Mayan culture into four basic periods: The Pre-Classic, the Classic, the Terminal Classic, and the Post-Classic. The Pre-Classic period has three further divisions called the Early Pre-Classic (2000-1000 BCE), Middle Pre-Classic (1000-300 BCE), and Late Pre-Classic (300 BCE-250 CE). These dates have been determined by carbon dating. As the Mayan civilization evolved, a number of different subcultures were formed which are listed below in ascending chronological order (beginning with the Late Pre-classic/Late Formative).

300 BCE-200 CE: Late Pre-Classic or Late Formative

East: (Maya and Isthmian) Kaminajuyu, Izapa, Chiapa de Corzo, Takalik

Central Mexico: short-lived Cuicuilco and the beginning of Teotihuacan

West: Mexcala, Colima, Chupicuaro

Oaxaca: Monte Alban II

200 CE-600 CE: Early Classic

East: Maya

Central Mexico: dominant Teotihuacan, Cholula (Teotihuacan collapses c. 650 CE)

Oaxaca: Monte Alban III

Gulf Coast: Remojadas

West: Mezcala, Colima, Nayarit, Jalisco, Michoacan

600 CE-900 CE: Late Classic

East: Maya

Central Mexico: Cacaxtla, Xochicalco, and other small towns

Oaxaca: Monte Alban IV

Gulf Coast: Veracruz/El Tajin, Huasteca

West: Colima, Nayarit, Jalisco, Michoacan

800 CE-1050 CE: TERMINAL CLASSIC

East: Many Mayan cities fall; Yucatan flourishes, including Chichen Itza, Uxmal, Kabah, Labna, Sayil, and Tulum

The rest of Mesoamerica suffers a general collapse.

900 CE-1350 CE: EARLY POST-CLASSIC

East: Chichen is abandoned in 1000 CE. Mayapan and other minor city-states try to preserve the magnificent achievements of the Mayan Empire.

Oaxaca: Mixteca (Monte Alban V)

Central Mexico/Puebla: Cholula re-occupation, Tula Hidalgo

1350 CE-1520 CE: LATE POST-CLASSIC

East: Independent, small Mayan city-states

Central Mexico: Mexica/Aztec hegemony

Other states: Cholula, Tlaxcala.

The rest of Mesoamerica contains civilized states; many are dominated by the Aztecs.

1520 CE-1560 CE: EARLY COLONIAL

East: In the central Peten region of Guatemala, the Mayan kingdom of Tayasal remained independent of Spanish control until 1697.

Cortes conquers most of New Spain; he completely destroys the Aztec culture and enslaves the population. Hundreds of churches are built.

Although information is scarce, there are archeologists, scientists, and historians who have pieced together a fairly accurate understanding of the Mayan culture. Let's take a closer look at the development of the Mayan civilization during each of the four basic time periods.

Pre-Classic Period

Most of the development of Mayan cities began in the latter part of this period. Recent archeological discoveries place the Mayan occupation at Cuello in Belize as early as 2000 BCE. Significantly, Cuello is the place where the Mayan Long Count Calendar was first discovered. As previously mentioned, the Mayas may not have created the first calendar system. There were other Mesoamerican cultures that used calendars, and the Mayas were able to improve upon them. The Mayan Long Count Calendar predates the earliest historical records as it begins on August 11, 3114 BCE and ends on December 21, 2012.

As the Long Count Calendar was evolving, there were important villages being built in the Mayan lowlands between 900-800 BCE:

 + Nakbe
 + El Mirador
 + Cival
 + San Bartolo

During this period, the Mayas traded jade and obsidian and established trade routes to Peten and the Pacific Lowlands. They also began growing cacao (cocoa plant) in 600 BCE which they used and traded. The centers of production were the following:

 + Izapa
 + Takalik Abaj
 + Chocolá

During this time, the Mayas built ball courts, which were similar to those used by the Olmecs. A more in-depth discussion of the ball courts and the ball game are presented in Chapter 4.

Classic Period

Most urban construction took place during the Classic period (250 CE–900 CE). The Mayas created monumental inscriptions representing significant intellectual and artistic development. It was during this period that Mayan cities began to form. Their independent city-states were as follows:

+ Tikal
+ Palenque
+ Copán
+ Calakmul
+ Dos Pilas
+ Uaxactun
+ Altun Ha
+ Bonampak

The ruins of King Pacal's Palenque, from an elevated view

In the Northern Lowlands, the following city-states have been discovered:

- Oxkintok
- Chunchucmil
- Early Uxmal

During the Classic Period, the Mayas occupied more than 100,000 square miles of the Yucatan Lowlands. Their hierarchical structure included great lords and an elite class. They ruled over fifty independent states that included tens of thousands of farming villages. Like the Olmecs, the Mayas were great traders with extensive trade routes throughout the Valley of Oaxaca.

Also during this period, the Mayan kings left their legacy in the form of intricately carved stone stelae to commemorate their accessions and ancestors. These men were powerful kings who ruled over large and vibrant communities. "They built great cities and trading centers around palaces, plazas, and pyramids. Grandiose public buildings, which were adorned with stone and stucco sculptures of deities and mythical creatures of lords conducting important ceremonies…" (Brian M. Fagen, *Kingdoms of Gold, Kingdoms of Jade,* Thames & Hudson, 1991).

As with other Mesoamerican cultures, the early Mayan empire lacked distinct borders. The Mayas lived in the area of the Olmecs near Veracruz and Tabasco. Since there were no formal boundaries between city-states, there was much overlapping of cultures in the various regions. At many archeological sites in Guatemala, the distinctive features of Olmec and Mayan artifacts have been found in close proximity.

During the Classic Period, the development of urban centers in the Mayan regions flourished. Large scale construction projects were built during this Period and included the addition of inscriptions and hieroglyphs on monuments. The Southern Lowlands experienced a surge in artistic and intellectual development. Great strides

were made in the design of palaces, pyramids, and carved stone slabs, called *tetun* or "stone trees" by the Mayas. Hieroglyphs on the tetun depicted their rulers, genealogy, and military conquests.

TERMINAL CLASSIC PERIOD

The Terminal Classic Period is generally considered to mark the beginning of the end of the Mayan culture. The great city-states that had grown and thrived throughout the previous centuries began to erode as the common people struggled for survival, searching for food sources and rebelling against the elite class.

This time period (800-1050 CE) actually overlaps the Late Classic Period (600-900 CE) and the Early Post–Classic Period (900-1350 CE). It was a time of turbulence as the Mesoamerican cultures began to collapse.

At this time, the Mayas were still developing cities in the Northern part of their empire, while the Southern areas were experiencing a decline. The peak of Maya culture shifted to the North, to the Puuc Hills, centered at Uxmal. The Puuc architectural style is defined by the building styles seen there. The influence of Puuc style architecture at Chichén Itzá is seen most easily in the older Southern section, in the Nunnery Annex, the Iglesia, and in other small buildings in this area. Some Puuc style facades can be seen today in the older buildings where the outer building has fallen away, exposing the original façade beneath. The inner temple in El Castillo is also almost pure Puuc Mayan. Only 100 years after the collapse of the Southern and Central Mayan cities, the cities in the Puuc hills also collapsed, ending the Classic era.

Post-Classic Period

This Mayan period spanned from 900-1500 CE. According to archeological reports, Mayan cities had spread out like an urban sprawl. Most historians believe that the Terminal Classic period marks the beginning of demise of the Mayan culture, and the Post-Classic Period was filled with corruption and armed conflict throughout these large city-states.

However, recent excavations of Early Post-Classic communities (by the Belize Post-Classic Project) offer insights into the continuation of the Mayan culture after 900 CE. Evidence from sites such as Laguna de On and Caye Coco at Progresso Lagoon indicates that the Mayan civilization continued for over six centuries after its so-called 'collapse'. Therefore, it is possible that the Terminal Classic Period (800 CE-1050 CE) lasted through the Early and Late Post-Classic Periods (900-1520 CE), and didn't end until the Spanish Colonial Period of the 16th century (1520-560 CE).

The site of Lamanai is among the few examined sites of this period that exhibits continuous occupation from the Classic through the Post-Classic Periods. In support of this claim, the site

Depiction of war-like Mayas during Late Classic Period

of Lamanai exhibits continuous occupation from the Terminal Classic throughout the Post-Classic Periods.

After the collapse of the great city-states, the Mayas no longer built large monuments and stelae, and instead, focused on production and trade which resulted in greater prosperity for more people.

Chapter 2

THE MAYAS

The information presented thus far is generally accepted Mayan history. Despite the theories of anthropologists, historians, scholars, and scientists, no one has satisfactorily explained where the Mayas came from. We can only make assumptions about their socio-political structure, religion, economic structure, and daily life. Due to the destruction of books and codices, detailed information has yet to emerge on this subject. Unfortunately, the Spanish conquerors burned the Mayan, Aztec, and Toltec written accounts of their civilizations' histories, societies, and cultures. Because of this thoughtless destruction, only speculative theories remain as to why the great Mayan cities were abandoned in the 9th century CE. Furthermore, experts on Mayan history are perplexed by their disappearance and consider it to be a baffling archeological mystery.

INCIDENTS OF TRAVEL

In 1836, scholar John Lloyd Stephens developed a theory about the origins of the Mayan people. Stephens was a lawyer turned travel writer, who had achieved fame by describing his adventures in Egypt, Russia, and the Middle East in the 1830s. While in New York, he met Frederick Catherwood, a British architect and sketch artist, who had a gift for illustrating ancient ruins. These two men made a formidable writer/artist team. When they heard rumors of ancient temples deep in the Central American rain forest, they saw a chance for a good story.

Stephens and Catherwood discovered Mayan ruins at Copan after landing in British Honduras (present-day Belize). Both were astonished at their findings and spent two weeks mapping out the site. They surmised that it was built by some long forgotten people and could not believe that the ancient Mayas had lived there.

Eventually, Stephens and Catherwood made their way to Palenque and Uxmal. According to Stephens, they visited a total of 44 sites containing Mayan ruins. They reached Palenque in 1840 and recorded many details of the ruins they found, including Temple of the Inscriptions, Temple of the Cross, Temple of the Sun, and Temple of the Foliated Cross.

Stephens and Catherwood made an important contribution to Mayan history by writing and illustrating the details of several ancient sites. Stephens continued his investigations for another year and returned to the Yucatan several times to collect additional information for his next two books, *Incidents of Travel in Central America, Chiapas and Yucatan, Vols. 1 & 2* (1841), and *Incidents of Travel in Yucatan, Vols. 1 & 2* (1843).

In 1842, Stephens and Catherwood provided the first written accounts of Labna, an important ceremonial center in the Puuc Hills region of the Yucatan Peninsula. This site is comparatively small and compact, but among the ruins is a notable two-story palace known

Gateway at Labna (also known as Labna Vault),
as drawn by Frederick Catherwood

as *El Palacio*. It is one of the longest contiguous structures in the Puuc region. Leading into the palace, a ceremonial road called a *sacbe* extends out to an elaborately decorated gateway arch (*El Arco*). This structure has a height of 19.7 ft. and width of 9.8 ft. and has well-preserved bas-reliefs. There is also an arch that is not an entrance to the city, but a passageway between public areas.

Next to this gateway stands *El Mirador*, a pyramid-like structure surmounted by a temple, which is on the same site as the Temple of the Columns. The structural designs and motifs represent an architectural style named after the region (Puuc). It connotes well-cut stone patterns and masks of the long-nosed rain-god *Chaac*. This site was built during the Terminal Classic era, and inscribed in the palace is a Mayan date that corresponds to 862 CE.

Stephens was intrigued with the quiet structures in Mayan cities and thought of them as looking "grim and mysterious." He decided to dedicate the rest of his life to studying the accomplishments of this advanced civilization and became known as "the Father of Mayan studies." Stephens said, "In the romance of the world's history, nothing ever impressed me so forcibly than the spectacle of this once great and lovely city, overturned, desolate, and lost. It did not even have a name to distinguish it" (John Lloyd Stephens, *Incidents of Travel in Central America*, 1841).

THE MAYAS AND THE LOST TRIBES OF ISRAEL

In his book, Stephens quotes Francisco Antonio de Fuentes y Guzman, a writer who documented the history of the ancient Guatemalan kingdom, who contends that the Quiche Maya are connected to the Twelve Tribes of Israel.

Fuentes y Guzman (1643 – 1700) wrote:

According to the grandson of the last king of the Quiches, the Toltecs were outcast Israelites, who were given freedom by Moses from the tyranny of Pharaoh. After crossing the Red Sea, they became idolaters. To escape the continued reproofs of Moses, they strayed away and, under the leadership of a man named Tanub, drifted from continent to continent until they came to a place they called the Seven Caverns, which was a part of the kingdom of Mexico. They founded the city of Tula, in the now state of Hidalgo, 60 miles north of Teotihuacan. From Tanub, the story goes, sprang the ruling Elites of the Toltec and the Quiche Mayas (*History of Guatemala*).

This speculative theory is worth mentioning because, when it comes to the origins of the Maya, all the stories relating to the origins of the Quiche Maya are a bit strange. With that said, let's take a look at another hypothesis that attempts to link the Maya to a great civilization from the East.

Possible Link to the Phoenicians

There are many controversial theories relating to the development of Mayan civilization. As discussed, the Olmec migration across the Bering-Strait represents the historical narrative. However, there are several indications that point to the possibility of cross oceanic travels by various advanced civilizations. The following evidence cannot be ignored while tracing the roots of the Quiche Mayas:

- Ruins of Phoenician ships found in Paraguay and Brazil;
- Carvings in Bolivia similar to the Indus script of pre-India;
- Peyote (derived from American cactus) found in burial chambers of Egyptian kings;
- Pottery in Peru with similar figurines to Phoenician pottery;
- The existence of pyramids in both hemispheres and;
- Similarities with Egyptian calendars, hieroglyphics, mathematics, and astronomical readings.

There is also speculation that the Phoenicians were the earliest navigators of the world. Some believe they were the first advanced civilization to visit Palenque and Uxmal (where they designed temples and pyramids). The histories of the fourth Quetzalcoatl and the Maya reveal that the Chontal Maya (usually referred to as an indigenous people) had all the characteristics of the ancient Phoenicians. They were known by the word, Putun, which has similar consonants as that of "Punt" or "Pont," and which may derive from Punic and Phoenician. This group has been identified with the Itza who are a Guatemalan ethnic group of Maya affiliation.

Interestingly, author Charles Gallenkamp offers the following observations about a possible connection between the Phoenicians and the Putun:

> J. Eric Thompson, who studied this problem [who the Itza really were] in-depth, identified the Itza as a group called the Putun or Chontal, a Maya-speaking people who inhabited the coast of Tabasco and Campeche. Famed as long distance traders and seamen, the Putun expanded into Yucatan and settled at Chichen Itzas around 981 CE, bringing with them many earmarks of Mexican culture. When Quetzalcoatl and his Toltec followers arrived at Chichen Itza from Tula in 987, they were cordially received by the Putun-Itza, whose own Mexican affinities encouraged them to enter into an alliance with the Toltecs (*Maya: The Riddle and Rediscovery of a Lost Civilization.* NY: Viking Penguin, 1985).

Some anthropologists believe that the Putun-Itza influence was extensive throughout the Mayan empire. They contend that close commercial ties existed between the Putins, Toltecs, and other groups in Central Mexico. According to Gallenkamp:

> As warriors and merchants they were extremely aggressive, and throughout the Post-Classic Period they controlled trade routes that extended from the Gulf Coast of Mexico around the Yucatan Peninsula to Honduras. It is also probable that the Toltec influences so firmly imprinted on the ruins of Chichen Itza may be attributable to the Putun. Quite possibly, they either fostered incursions into Yucatan by the Toltecs (with whom the Putun regularly traded), or they were allied with Toltec warriors brought in by the Putun-Itza to protect their far flung trading networks (p. 168).

The Yucatan was not the only scene of Putun incursions that moved them into the territory of the Mayas. With the Putun came new, sophisticated types of ceramics known as the "fine orange and fine gray," which were widely traded in many areas. They also incised strange "Mexicanized" portraits of their elite onto stone monuments at Seibal, which represent Putun lords who seized control of the city. Gallenkamp continues:

> Among the invading armies, were well-organized military orders using the Eagle and Jaguar as their symbols. Newly introduced weapons included cotton armor, atlatls, slings, and obsidian-edged swords, and there was an increased emphasis on militarism in all phases of political and religious life. Human sacrifice began to be practiced on a scale never before approached in the Classic Period, with the ruthless Toltec-Itza soldiers assuming a vital ritualistic function as providers of captives for sacrificial purposes (p. 169-170).

This subject is ripe for further research and investigation. In the future, if archeologists are able to establish a verifiable connection between the Putun and the Phoenicians, a new era of Mesoamerican-Transatlantic scholarship will be recognized by the academic community.

THEORIES FROM THE POPOL VUH

To further support the claim that travelers from the East visited the Mayan empire, there are references found in the sacred Mayan text, the *Popol Vuh*. This book traces the travels of these early explorers as they sailed eastward across the Atlantic Ocean. Other tribal nations have similar stories about how they "crossed a great body of water" to reach their new homelands (Herman L. Hoeh, *Compendium of World History*, Vol. II, 1969).

According to the *Popol Vuh*:

> They also multiplied there in the East. They all lived together; they existed in great numbers and walked there in the East. There they were then, in great numbers, the black man and the white man, many of many classes, men of many tongues...the speech of all was the same. They did not invoke wood, or stone, and they remembered the word of the Creator and the Maker. [The Mayas] came from the East.... They left there, from a great distance...and crossed the sea.

The *Popol Vuh* also states that humans were first created in the East and lived there in darkness. Subsequently, the ancestors of the Maya left the East "by crossing the sea in a fleet of seven vessels carrying many companies; and they sailed along the Gulf of Mexico to its farthest westward point; finally at Panuco, Veracruz, the people disembarked" (Stephen C. Jett, *Pre-Columbian Transoceanic Contacts*, n.p., 1983).

From Panuco, the Mayas were led by priests, who carried their symbols of rank to Tula. According to the legend, "they walked with their gods, and their gods with them."

In this chapter, various suppositions have been presented on the origins of the Mayas. However, even the remotest possibility that the Mayas may have originated from a civilization that lived across the Atlantic Ocean is a possibility worth exploring.

Chapter 3

RELIGION

Mayan rituals and ceremonies were very closely associated with celestial and terrestrial cycles. The Mayan priests were responsible for interpreting these cycles and prophesying the future based on interrelationships between their calendars. They also had to choose an appropriate time when the conditions in the heavens were just right for performing certain religious ceremonies.

The Mayas understood the importance of offering sacrifices to their gods. Bloodletting and human sacrifice were common rituals among the Mayas until their god Kukulcan prohibited this practice. Their gods displayed different characteristics and held domain over various aspects of nature. Although their religion was polytheistic, their "god of all gods" was the monotheistic Hanab Ku (the Ultimate Reality), followed by Gucametz (Creator), who is closely related to Kukulcan (also known as Quetzalcoatl among the Aztecs). Other important gods include Itzamna (another Creator god), Huracan (god of wind, storm, and fire), Chaac (rain god), Kinich Ahau (sun deity), and Ix Chel (goddess of the moon). A pantheon of over one hundred Mesoamerican gods and goddesses were included in this Spiritual hierarchy which is reminiscent of the mythologies of Egypt, Greece, and Rome. The Mayan gods and goddesses were divided between nine levels of the Underworld and thirteen levels of the Upper World. Interestingly, the Mayan royalty believed they had descended from the gods.

Spiritual Beliefs

According to a modern Mayan teacher, Alom Ahau Tze'ec Ba'lam (aka. Don Rios), the spiritual beliefs of present-day Mayas accurately reflect the core teachings of their ancestors. He writes:

> The Maya believe that all things are living and vibrating, and that we must as humans maintain respect for all creation. We do not condone any type of aggression toward anyone or Mother Earth.
>
> Our humble teachings are easy to assimilate and integrate into one's life, allowing us insight and understanding of our place, space, and time in the cosmos.
>
> We are co-creators of our lives and of our health. We as humans need to come back into the understanding that all things are possible and feel the power of our connection to the Creator and Maker. We then have the ability to supersede all limitations of the mind and body.
>
> The concept of living differs in the Mayan World as well. We believe that we are spirits here for the physical experience of life. Therefore, it is both our gift and our responsibility to enjoy life and live fully. We follow the principles of the Chilam Ba'lam; the sacred book of the Jaguar to help guide us on this path of life.
>
> In the Mayan World, we live our lives in harmony with the world that surrounds us. When we are in need of healing, we simply turn to our environment for help. With the use of herbs, stones, and nature, we can return to a state of balance in our lives.
>
> We use many techniques that have been passed down through the generations to recreate health for ourselves and loved ones. Healing teas, salves, and ceremonies are part of the healing process (http://homeofthemaya.tripod.com/ viewed March 23, 2009).

As reflected above, present-day Mayas are devoted to the principles of the *Chilam Ba'lam*. The word "chilam" translates as "interpreter of the gods" and "ba'lam" means "jaguar". This set of books was named after their prophet "Chilam" who predicted the coming of strangers from across the ocean and the establishment of a new religion. The *Chilam Ba'lam* was originally written in the Mayan language, and its writings encapsulate the beliefs and priorities of an advanced civilization. These texts contain historical, cultural, and religious information that offer scholars important insights into the minds of the Quiche Mayas (natives of the Post-Classic period). Significantly, there are four types of prophecies contained in the Chilam Ba'lam: daily, yearly, cycles of 20 years (katun), and cycles referring to the return of Kukulcan (Quetzalcoatl).

POPOL VUH (BOOK OF THE COMMUNITY)

The *Popol Vuh* is a 17th century sacred text that is based on an earlier lost manuscript from the 1500s CE. It reveals the history, culture, cosmology, and religious ideals of the Mayas and the Quiche Kingdom.

The beginning of the *Popol Vuh* corresponds with the basic creation story in the *Book of Genesis*, but then takes a different turn to tell the story of how human beings were created. As the book begins, the gods are having a difficult time creating the first people, finally succeeding on the fourth attempt. Next, there is a story about Hero Twins who invent a famous ballgame and then have a

The Popol Vuh

confrontation with the Lords of the Underworld. The book is filled with delightful and tragic myths of this kind that form the basis of Mayan theology. Additionally, there is an appreciation for corn as the centerpiece of the Mayan diet, along with detailed descriptions of the gods, the names of royal families, their lineages, and dialogues between the gods and the first people.

The *Popol Vuh* states:

> Then the Creator and the Maker asked them: "What do you think of your condition? Do you not see? Do you not hear? Are not your speech and manner of walking good? Look, then! Contemplate the world, look [and see] if the mountains and the valleys appear! Try, then, to see!" they said to [the four first men].
>
> And immediately they [the four first men] began to see all that was in the world. Then they gave thanks to the Creator and the Maker: "We really give you thanks, two and three times! We have been created, we have been given a mouth and a face, we speak, and we hear, we think, and walk; we feel perfectly, and we know what is far and what is near" (*Popol Vuh*, Part 3, Chapter 2).

This excerpt tells the story of how self-consciousness was awakened within the first four Mayan men. Their names are: Balam-Quitzé, Balam-Acab, Mahucutah, and Iqui-Balam. Interestingly, this story of awakening is similar to the biblical tale of Adam and Eve when their eyes open after eating the forbidden fruit. Furthermore, just as Adam wakes up from a deep sleep to find Eve beside him, the four Mayan men awaken to find four women beside them as well. Their names are: Cahá-Paluna—wife of Balam-Quitzé; Chomihá—wife of Balam-Acab; Tzununihá—wife of Mahucutah; and Caquixahá—wife of Iqui-Balam.

The *Popol Vuh* is one of few surviving sacred texts written by the Mayas and is the basis of many Mesoamerican cultural and spiritual beliefs. The *Popol Vuh* also contains cosmic concepts, cultural traditions, and a chronological record of historical chiefs and kings up to the year 1550. The original copy was found by Father Ximenez, a Franciscan monk, who lived in the ancient Guatemala Mayan capital city of Chichicastenango.

Father Ximenez transcribed the *Popol Vuh* into Spanish in circa 1700 CE. This was an important find because there are only a small number of early Mesoamerican mythological texts. The mythology of the Quiche Mayas as told in the *Popol Vuh* matches the imagery found in Mayan art.

The story begins with the Mayan gods creating the Universe and ends with the radiant splendor of gods establishing the Quiche Kingdom in the Guatemala Highlands. Most of the book explains the foundation and history of the Quiche kingdom, including stories of the royal family and legendary gods who ruled by divine right. The following is a summary of the four main parts of the *Popol Vuh*:

PART 1

+ Gods create the world.
+ Gods create the first wooden humans who are imperfect and emotionless.
+ Gods destroy the first humans in a "resin" flood, and they become monkeys.
+ Twin diviners Hunahpu and Xbalanque destroy the arrogant Vucub-Caquix, Zipacna, and Cabracan.

PART 2

+ Diviners Xpiyacoc and Xmucane beget brothers.
+ Hun Hunahpu and Xbaquiyalo beget Monkey Twins: Hun Batz and Hun Chouen.
+ Cruel Xibalba lords kill the brothers Hun Hunahpu and Vucub Hunahpu.
+ Hun Hunahpu and Xquic beget Hero Twins: Hunahpu and

Xbalanque.

+ Hero Twins defeat the Xibalba houses of Gloom, Knives, Cold, Jaguars, Fire, and Bats.

Part 3

+ The first four "real" people are created: Balam-Quitze, Jaguar Night, Naught, and Wind Jaguar.
+ Tribes descend; they speak the same language and travel to Tulan Zuiva.
+ The tribes' languages became confused, and the tribes disperse (similar to the Biblical story of the Tower of Babel).
+ Tohil is recognized as a god and demands live sacrifices. Later on, he is hidden away.

Part 4

+ Tohil affects Earth lords through priests, but his dominion destroys the Quiche.
+ Priests try to abduct tribes for sacrifices, but they are met with resistance.
+ Quiche finds Gumarcah where Gucumatz (Quetzalcoatl, the feathered serpent lord) raises them to power.
+ Gucumatz institutes elaborate rituals.
+ Genealogies of the tribes are given.

This mythology has a connection to the Pre-Classic Mayas, as depicted in the San Bartolo murals. Certain images seem to come directly from the *Popol Vuh*, such as the Mayan Hero Twins (in particular the shooting of Vucub-Caquix and the restoration of the twins' dead father) and the Howler Monkey gods.

QUETZALCOATL

The legend of Quetzalcoatl is well known to the Mexican people. It tells an interesting story about a plumed serpent who became a god-man to the Mayas. Quetzalcoatl was revered as a great mystical leader and first appeared to the people of Teotihuacan near the area around Mexico City. He divulged great secrets to the Mayas and gave them advanced knowledge in the arts and sciences. Eventually, he became their ruler and led the city into an era of prominence and prosperity. Years later, he fell in disgrace for violating his own laws and set himself on fire. According to the mythology, he rose in flames to become the planet Venus and vowed to return one day to his people.

Quetzalcoatl's departure was the work of his old enemy, Tezcatlipoca, who wanted Mayas to change their sacrificial offerings from flowers, jade, and butterflies to bloodier sacrifices. Tezcatlipoca tricked Quetzalcoatl by getting him drunk and then holding up a mirror that showed Tezcatlipoca's cruel face. Believing that he was looking at his own imperfect image, Quetzalcoatl decided to leave the world and threw himself onto a funeral pyre.

Another version of the myth says that Quetzalcoatl sailed east on a raft of serpents. As his body burned, birds flew forth from the flames, and his heart went up into the heavens to become Venus, the morning and evening star.

After this event, all priests in the Toltec cult were given the title of Quetzalcoatl. One such priest by the name of Ce Acatl Topiltzin rose to power and proclaimed himself as the second coming of Quetzalcoatl. In 968 CE, he became king of the Toltec people and reigned for

Quetzalcoatl

decades. He is credited with building the Toltec capital of Tula. Eventually, in like manner to the first Quetzalcoatl, Ce Acatl Topiltzin was disposed of by his enemies and escaped on a raft of snakes sailing east. He vowed to return one day to rule his people. Interestingly, it is this snake reference that provided the inspiration for artists depicting Quetzalcoatl as emerging, or being "reborn" as he emerges, from the mouth of a serpent. The raft of snakes carried Quetzalcoatl east and south across the Gulf of Mexico to a Yucatan beach.

During this time, the Mayan people were also expecting the return of their plumed serpent god, Kukulcan, who, just like Quetzalcoatl, promised to return to rule his people after being forced to leave. To this day, many Mesoamerican people believe he will return home in the future, possibly in 2012.

According to legend, Quetzalcoatl was buried under the Temple of the Dwarf, where he remains to this day. Although a burial plot has yet to be discovered, the legend says that his spirit is buried in the roots of the El Tule Tree. This tree is located in Santa Maria, El Tule, Oaxaca, and is said to be the oldest tree in North America (2,000 years old).

El Tule Tree, Santa Maria El Tule, Oaxaca

Temple of the Feathered Serpent at the Ciudadela complex in Teotihuacan with inset detail of Feathered Serpent head

Based on the iconography of the feathered serpent at Teotihuacan, Xochicalco, Chichen Itza, Tula, and Tenochtitlan, historian David Carrasco argues that this deity was the patron god of urban centers, culture, and civilization.

From a translation of the Chimalpopoca Codex:

Quetzalcoatl, Our Prince, had brought religious reform to Tula. He believed that human sacrifice had to be stopped and so it was done. But others were not pleased, those who had followed Tezcatlipoca were angry. Their god had demanded the nectar of human blood as his tribute. Thus those who followed Tezcatlipoca had plotted to do away with Our Prince.

Death, unfortunately, was not to be. For in death, they believed that Quetzalcoatl would gain more followers, and then his teachings could not be silenced. No, they sought to destroy him in such a manner as to discredit his message, which would be more painful than death. Hence, they set out to trick Our Prince. They held before him, one day, a mirror, and to his astonishment Quetzalcoatl had seen how old he was. Falling into despair, he wondered what to do.

His enemies then said to him that they could make him young again, and produced for him a cure. Believing this was his salvation, Quetzalcoatl had taken this offering. But this cure was pulque, which his lips had never touched before. The pulque racing in his blood caused Quetzalcoatl to act not like himself. He had relations with a woman that he would have never committed before.

And when word spread about Tula, the people were shocked and ashamed. Seeing his people's faces and hearts, Our Prince decided to flee. Across the land, he and some of his loyal followers went, until they reached Tlillan Tlapallan where Our Prince was then no more. And so greatly did (the Toltecs) believe in their priest, Quetzalcoatl,

And so greatly obedient,
And given to the things of their god were they.
And so fearful of god
All believed in Quetzalcoatl when he left Tula...
And so much did they trust Quetzalcoatl,
That they went with him, they entrusted upon him
Their wives, their children, their sick ones.
They stood up, they set off,
The old men, the old women,
No one ceased to obey,
All set off.
Suddenly, he went towards the center of the sea,
Towards the land, and there he disappeared.
He, our prince, Quetzalcoatl ...

Chapter 4

MAYAN ACCOMPLISHMENTS

Between 200 BCE and 900 CE, the Mayan empire flourished and prospered. The Mayas made major contributions in mathematics, astronomy, writing, engineering, architecture, and urban planning. They created a huge empire of cities, pyramids, palaces, and temples that were decorated with fine art, encrusted with gems, and plated with gold. Their culture rivals the great civilization of Egypt, and they left behind many artistic and scientific remnants. Many of these items are indicative of an extremely advanced civilization.

WRITING AND LITERACY

The Mayan writing symbols are referred to as *hieroglyphs* because of their resemblance to ancient Egyptian hieroglyphics. They are a combination of phonetic pictographs and logograms that are often classified as *logographic* or *logosyllabic* (with syllabic signs playing a significant role). It is the only writing system of the Pre-Columbian New World that is known to represent the spoken language of its community. In total, the script includes more than a thousand different glyphs, although some are rarely used and others are confined to particular localities. At any one time, no more than 500 glyphs were in use, and over 200 variations had a phonetic or syllabic interpretation.

The earliest inscriptions of Mayan script dates back to circa 300 BCE. However, these writings are preceded by several other writing systems that were developed in Mesoamerica by the Zapotecs and the Olmecs. Significantly, a pre-Mayan writing system known as "Epi-Olmec script" represents a transitional script between Olmec

Mayan Hieroglyphs on Codex

and Mayan writing, but scholars are not in agreement regarding its validity.

On January 5, 2006, *National Geographic* published its findings on Mayan writings that date back to 400 BCE. If this is true, the Mayan writing system is one of the oldest ever found in Mesoamerica (along with Zapotec). Subsequently, the Mayas developed their script into a more complex and complete form that surpassed all others in the Americas. Even after many Mayan centers went into decline or were completely abandoned, the skill and knowledge of Mayan writing persisted among segments of the population. The early Spanish conquistadors indicated in their records that the Mayas could still read and write the script. Unfortunately, the Spanish displayed little interest in Mayan writing skills, and the knowledge needed for deciphering their hieroglyphics was lost within a few generations.

Mayan Writing Tablet

CODICES

In excess of 10,000 individual texts have been recovered from inscriptions on stone monuments, stelae, and ceramic pottery. The Mayas also produced texts painted on a form of paper manufactured from processed maguey. This paper is now known by its Nahuatl name, *amatl*. It is typically bound as a single continuous sheet that folds into pages of equal width, concertina-style, which produces a codex that allows for writing on both sides.

Shortly after the Spanish conquest, all the codices were believed to be burned by zealous Spanish priests (most notably, Bishop Diego de Landa). Fortunately, there are three reasonably intact Mayan codices that survived. They are known as the Madrid, Dresden, and Paris codices. Additionally, a few pages remain from a fourth text known as the *Grolier Codex*, but its authenticity is in dispute.

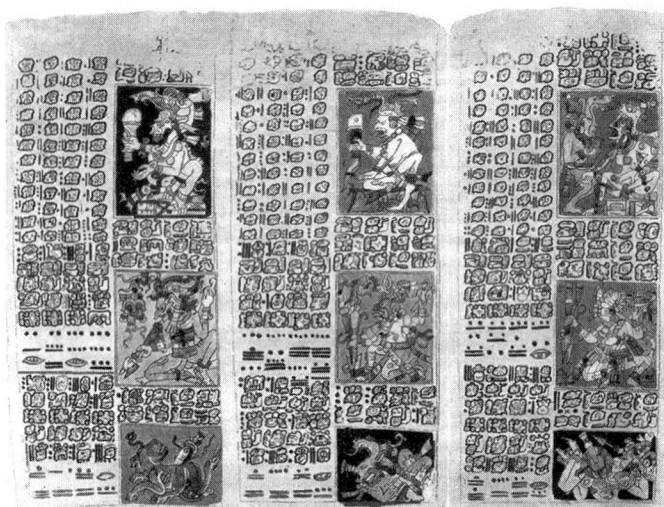

The Dresden Codex

Today's archeological digs at Mayan sites often reveal new fragments from codices, along with rectangular lumps of plaster, which were also former Mayan texts. Unfortunately, many of these tantalizing remains are too severely damaged to read the inscriptions. In reference to the few extant Mayan writings, Michael D. Coe, a prominent linguist and epigrapher at Yale University, asserts:

> Our knowledge of ancient Mayan thought must represent only a tiny fraction of the whole picture, for of the thousands of books in which the full extent of their learning and ritual was recorded, only four have survived to modern times (as though all that posterity knew of ourselves were to be based upon three prayer books and "Pilgrim's Progress") (Michael D. Coe, *The Maya*, Thames and Hudson, 4th ed., 1987).

With advances in the translation of glyphic writing, archeologists have uncovered additional information about the ancient Mayas. Most surviving pre-Columbian Mayan writings come from stelae and other stone inscriptions found at Mayan sites. Many of these areas were already abandoned before the Spanish arrived. The translated inscriptions on the stelae usually speak of dynasties, conquests, and wars, alliances and raids, and the genealogy of the rulers of the time. There are also inscriptions revealing information about the lifestyle and importance of Mayan women, and funeral pottery with hieroglyphs was found which depicted scenes of the afterlife.

WRITING TOOLS

Although archeological records do not provide examples, Mayan art shows that writing was done with brushes made with animal hair and quills. Codices were usually written in black ink with red highlights, which gave rise to the name for the Mayan territory as the "land of red and black".

Mayan plate with image of a scribe writing on a codex,
Classic period, 672-830 CE, from Nakbé, Guatemala

Court Scribe

Court Scribes

Scribes held a prominent position in the community. Mayan art depicts rulers as scribes with pen bundles in their headdresses, indicating that they were able to write. Additionally, many rulers in Mayan art were found holding writing tools, such as shell or clay inkpots. However, literacy was not widespread, and was usually confined to the ruling parties and the elite.

Mathematics and the Discovery of Zero

Like other Mesoamerican civilizations, the Mayas used base-20 and base-5 numbering systems. The Pre-Classic Mayas and their neighbors independently developed these methods for various types of calculations. Remarkably, many inscriptions show far-off dates into the hundreds of millions of years that contain so many digits it takes several lines to represent them.

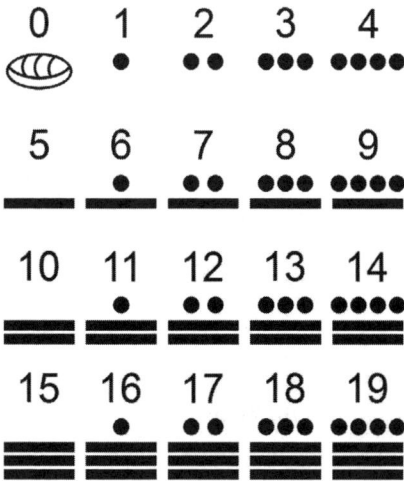

Mesoamerican Counting System

THE NUMBER 20

There are 206 "powers-of-twenty" words in Yucatec that are known to date (Floyd G. Lounsbury, "Maya Numeration, Computation, and Calendrical Astronomy," *Dictionary of Scientific Biography*, 1978). Mayan numbering methods use dots for units up to 4, and bars for 5s (up to fifteen). The bar-and-dot system is not limited to the Mayan region as it is also found in the Oaxaca Valley and the Olmec region. Twenties, four-hundreds, eight-thousands, and higher numbers are represented by symbols that are positioned above the base position. Each grouping has a place position in the base system, and several hieroglyphs use the zero as a symbol for unoccupied places (using a shell sign). Additionally, the names of Mayan numerical units go up to 64,000,000, and Stela F at Quirigua refers to a date that is over 90 million years ago.

In the Aztec system, numbers 1-19 are represented by dots, the 20s by flags, 400s by tree-like figures, and 8,000s by pouches or sacks. A variety of other numbering systems in the Mayan codices follow a similar pattern to those used by the Aztecs.

The Long Count Calendar uses the value of zero as a position marker within its vigesimal (base 20) number system. A shell glyph was used as the symbol for zero for Long Count dates. The oldest one known is found on Stela C from Tres Zapotes, with a date of 32 BCE. This is perhaps the oldest use of "zero" in the Western Hemisphere.

Long Count Calendar

Unlike our use of a single calendar today, the Mayas had different calendars for many practical uses (agricultural, commercial, etc.) while seeing all time as "a meshing of spiritual cycles." Most of their calendars were short, ranging from 260 days (Tzolk'in) to 365 days (Haab'). The Tzolk'in and Haab' calendars together comprised the Calendar Round, which could cover 52 years; but even that length was too limiting for the Mayas (Judge, 2009).

Tzolk'in and Haab'

Their solution for measuring extensive periods of time was the creation of the Long Count Calendar, which covers 5,125 years. The Mayas started their Long Count Calendar on a date they refer to as the "Birth of Venus." Based on a unit of 20 (rather than the modern base 10 system of counting), the Long Count Calendar could accurately pinpoint historical dates. However, the Mayas also used 13 as a root of their mathematical system. The two numbers (20 and 13) are used in interpreting the Long Count Calendar.

Since the Long Count contains 5 ages of 5,125 years each, the completion of one full cycle, or thirteen baktuns, equals 25,625 years. Each of the 5 cycles was considered to be its own world or sun cycle. As depicted on the Mesoamerican Sun Stone, each world is ruled by one of the four elements (fire, wind, rain, or water).

The Long Count began on August 11, 3114 BCE and ends 5,125 years later on December 21, 2012 CE.

The Long Count dates are written with Mesoamerican numerals, as shown in the picture captioned "Mesoamerican Counting System" previously in this chapter. A dot represents a 1 while a bar equals 5. The shell glyph was used to represent the zero concept. The Long Count Calendar required the use of zero as a placeholder and was one of the earliest uses of the concept of zero in history.

The back of Stela C from Tres Zapotes described in Chapter 1, is inscribed with the second oldest Long Count date yet discovered. The numerals 7.16.6.16.18 translate to September 1, 32 BCE (Gregorian). The glyphs surrounding the date are one of few surviving examples of Epi-Olmec script. The Long Count dates are written vertically with the longest time period on top (i.e., b'ak'tun), followed by progressively smaller time periods and ending with the Mayan number for one day (k'in). Accordingly, as seen in the left column, the Long Count date shows Stela C at Tres Zapotes as: 7.16.6.16.18.

7	x 144000	= 1,008000 days (k'in)
16	x 7200	= 115,200 days (k'in)
6	x 360	= 2,160 days (k'in)
16	x 20	= 320 days (k'in)
18	x 1	= 18 days (k'in)
	Total Days	=1,125,698 days (k'in)

JDN correlations to the Maya creation date (after Thompson 1971, et. al.)		Martinez-Hernandez	584,281
Name	**Correlation**	GMT	584,283
Wilson	438,906	Thompson (Lounsbury)	584,285
Smiley	482,699	Pogo	588,626
Makemson	489,138	+2CR	622,243
Spinden	489,384	Kreichgauer	626,927
Teeple	492,662	+4CR	660,203
Dinsmoor	497,879	Hochleitner	674,265
-4CR	508,363	Schultz	677,723
-2CR	546,323	Ramos	679,108
Stock	556,408	Valliant	679,183
Goodman	584,280	Weitzel	774,078

The date on Stela C indicates that 1,125,698 days have passed since the origination of August 11, 3114 BCE, Julian day number 1,709,981, September 1, 32 BCE in the Gregorian calendar, or September 3rd, -31 in the Julian calendar with astronomical dating.

The earliest Long Count inscription yet discovered is on Stela 2 at Chiapa de Corzo, Chiapas, Mexico, showing a date of 36 BCE.

Of the six sites, three are on the Western edge of the Mayan homeland, and three are several hundred kilometers farther west. This finding leads most researchers to believe that the Long Count Calendar predates the Mayas themselves. As discussed earlier, it probably originated with the Olmecs: La Mojarra Stela 1, the Tuxtla Statuette, Tres Zapotes Stela C, and Chiapa Stela 2 are all

Archaeological Site	Name	Gregorian Date (based on August 11)	Long Count Digits	Location
Chiopa de Corzo	Stela 2	December 10, 36 BCE	7.16.3.2.13	Chiapas, Mexico
Tres Zapotes	Stela C	September 3, 32 BCE	7.16.6.16.18	Veracruz, Mexico
El Baúl	Stela 1	March 6, 37 CE	7.19.15.7.12	Guatemala
Abaj Takalik	Stela 5	May 20, 103 CE	8.3.2.10.15	"
"	"	June 6, 126 CE	8.4.5.17.11	"
La Mojarra	Stela 1	July 14, 156 CE	8.5.16.9.7	Veracruz, Mexico
"	"	May 22, 143 CE	8.5.3.3.5	"
Near La Majorra	Tuxtla Staunette	March 15, 162 CE	8.6.2.4.17	"

This table lists the six artifacts with the eight oldest Long Count dates

Stela 1 from La Mojarra

inscribed in an Epi-Olmec, not Mayan, style. On the other hand, El Baul Stela 2 was created in the Izapan style. The first unequivocally Mayan artifact is Stela 29 from Tikal, with the Long Count date of 292 BCE (8.12.14.8.15), dating more than 300 years after Stela 2 from Chiapa de Corzo.

List of the Start Dates for 16 Baktuns	
Long Count	Gregorian (including proleptic)
GMT (584283) correlation	
13.0.0.0.0	August 11, 3114 BCE
1.0.0.0.0	November 13, 2720 BCE
2.0.0.0.0	February 16, 2325 BCE
3.0.0.0.0	May 21, 1931 BCE
4.0.0.0.0	August 23, 1537 BCE
5.0.0.0.0	November 26, 1143 BCE
6.0.0.0.0	February 28, 748 BCE
7.0.0.0.0	June 3, 354 BCE
8.0.0.0.0	September 5, 41 CE
9.0.0.0.0	December 9, 435
10.0.0.0.0	March 13, 830
11.0.0.0.0	June 15, 1224
12.0.0.0.0	September 18, 1618
13.0.0.0.0	December 21, 2012
14.0.0.0.0	March 26, 2407
15.0.0.0.0	June 28, 2801

Various methods have been proposed for converting a Long Count date to a Western calendar date. These methods or correlations are generally based on dates from the Spanish conquest, for which both Long Count and Western dates are known with some accuracy. The commonly established way of expressing the correlation between the Mayan calendar and the Gregorian or Julian calendars is to add the number of days from the start of the Julian Period (Monday, January 1, 4713 BCE) to the Long Count's zero date or base date, which was 13.0.0.0.0. Another, and more common, method of correlation is the Goodman-Martinez-Thompson correlation (GMT correlation), which establishes the 13.0.0.0.0 creation date as September 6, 3114 BCE (Julian) or August 11, 3114 BCE (Gregorian), Julian day number (JDN) 584283.

According to the *Popol Vuh*, we are living in the Fourth World. The text describes the first three creations that the gods failed in making and the creation of the successful Fourth World, where men were placed. In Mayan Long Count, the previous creation ended at the start of a 13th baktun, on a long count of 12.19.19.17.19. Another 12.19.19.17.19 will occur on December 20, 2012, followed by the start of the 14th baktun, 13.0.0.0.0, on December 21, 2012.

The Mayan calendar is a system of three distinct calendars that are perfectly coordinated:

a) An astronomical calendar that begins on the date the sun passes in a perpendicular direction through the zenith, a day between the 24th and 26th of July each year. This calendar encompassed 365.2420 days and was used to fix the position of the solstices, equinoxes, revolutions of the planets, eclipse nodes, and other celestial phenomena. This calendar was the base reference used by Mayan astronomers to calculate astronomical events (using a minimum of 4 decimals). This calendar has a margin of error of 0.0002%, while the Gregorian calendar is 0.0003%. Apparently the difference is very small, but the Mayan calendar was invented long before the Gregorian, which has been in use only since 1582, shortly after the Spanish conquered Yucatan.

b) *Tzolk'in* in Mayan means "the distribution of the days." In a ceremony performed on the astronomical New Year, the astronomer/priests indicated the days on which the agricultural, labor, and religious ceremonies were to take place within the next 260 day cycle. According to Mayan sage Don Pascual:

Our Grandfathers left an extraordinary legacy to humanity, one that synthesizes all of the wisdom of the ancient world. It is the most useful and transcendent instrument for both individuals and nations because it gives us the information we need for full, harmonious self-realization. I am speaking of none other than the sacred Cholq'ij of Tzolkin calendar, the count of days (Barrios, *The Book of Destiny*, 2009).

In addition to referring to this 260-day calendar, *Tzolk'in* is also used to designate the most important calendar of the Mayas, the sacred almanac or the Sacred Round. This calendar was a combination of a cycle of 13-day numbers with a cycle of 20-day names (the k'in). Within every 365-day Haab' year, there always ran a 260-day Tzolk'in calendar.

c) The 365-day civil calendar or Haab' is often referred to as the Vague Year. It was composed of 18 months of 20 days each and one month of 5 days, called *uayeb*. The difference of one fourth of a day in regard to the astronomical calendar made a periodical correction necessary through methods foreseen by the Mayas. Within this calendar ran the Tun year, which was 360 days long and was used for calendric calculations. It has 18,890 single days, making a period of 52 years.

ASTRONOMY

The Mayas had an extremely advanced ability to calculate the movements of celestial bodies. Their charts display incredibly precise movements of the moon, sun, Venus, and orbital cycles of Earth. Their calculations are far superior to any other civilization working only with the naked eye. Along with other Mesoamerican civilizations, the Mayas measured the exact length of the solar year using their Vague Year Calendar. It is called *vague* because 365.25 solar days is not exactly correct. The Mayas knew that the fraction of .25

of a day (after 365) is not the actual length of the solar year. The correct calculation is 365.242216 days, so the Julian year is too long by .0078 days (11 minutes 14 seconds). This may not seem like a lot of time, but over the course of several centuries it adds up, and eventually, in the 16th century, the vernal equinox fell on March 11 instead of March 21. Consequently, in 1582 CE, Pope Gregory XIII adjusted the calendar by moving the date ahead by 11 days and added an extra day for leap years. The modern Gregorian calendar is more accurate, but will accumulate an extra day in 3,257 years.

In addition to their precise calculations of the movements of the sun, moon, and planets, the Mayas were masters of the stars. There is evidence suggesting that the Mayas were the only civilization to demonstrate knowledge of the Orion Nebula without the use of a telescope. Many Pre-Classic sites are aligned with the star Alcyone of the Pleiades and the constellation Eta Draconis (Draco). These astronomical markings are seen in La Blanca, Ujuxte, Monte Alto, and Takalik Abaj. Like the Egyptians who aligned the Pyramids at Giza with Orion's Belt, the Mayas were intent on pointing out the essential nature of Alcyone and the Pleiades. According to legend, they believed their civilization originated from this area of the galaxy.

The Mayas were also interested in zenith passages (when the sun is directly overhead). Since the latitude of their cities fell below the Tropic of Cancer, zenith passages occurred twice a year and were equidistant from the solstice. To represent the position of the overhead sun, the Mayas created the "Diving God." Interestingly, the Temple of the Diving God has an unusual figure above the doorway that appears to be diving headfirst to Earth. There are many theories about the meaning of these curious carvings which also appear at the Mayan site of Coba. The Diving God is also "the god descending" and is associated with the planet Venus. It is a popular symbolic motif in temple doorways at Tulum.

The *Dresden Codex* contains the highest concentration of astronomical phenomena, observations, and calculations of any of the surviving texts. This data contains detailed astronomical information on the various cycles of Venus. Therefore, it is important to review why Venus was of such great interest to Mayan astronomers.

The Venus Factor

Venus was the most important planet in Mayan astronomy. The Mayas were experts in charting the cycles of its rising as the "morning star" (Ah-Chicum-Ek') and setting as the "evening star" (Lamat). It was considered a "companion" to the sun, and the Mayas meticulously followed its transit cycles (periodic alignments with Earth and the sun). Yet, in most books on 2012, Venus is not given the attention it deserves.

Apparently, the symbolism of Venus is not as "dazzling" as the end of the Mayan Calendar on December 21, 2012. Therefore, contemporary writers tend to minimize the importance of Venus' transit cycle that will end on June 5-6, 2012. A transit of Venus occurs when it passes directly in front of the sun. This phenomenon is similar to the moon's passing in front of the sun during a solar eclipse. But unlike the moon that blocks the sun, Venus is only a tiny dot that crosses the disc of the sun in intermittent cycles of 105.5, 121.5 and 243 years.

The Mayas were fascinated with Venus, and they watched its daily movements. *The Dresden Codex* contains the most detailed information on its transits, conjunctions, and eclipses. The text includes an elaborate calendar system that measures the precise orbit of Venus and the various distances between the sun, Earth, and other planets.

Along with the 365 day Haab solar calendar, and 260 day Tzolkin ritual calendar, the Mayas were in awe of the helical rising (appearance at sunrise) of Venus. Additionally, their ceremonial centers were designed to align with the early morning passage of the sun and its "companion" Venus.

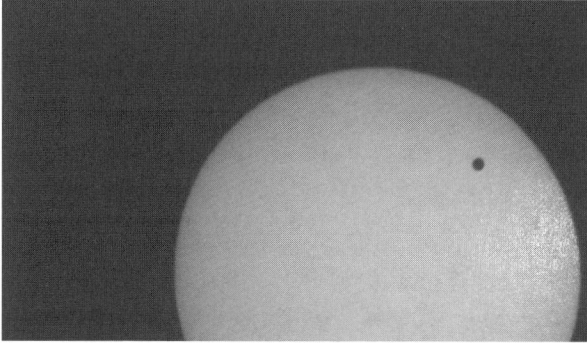

Transit of Venus 2004

The Venus transit of June 5-6, 2012 provides one of the most important clues for unraveling the Mayan mystery of 2012. Consequently, it is important to understand why our "sister" planet was sacred to the Mayas. According to myth, the Mayan god-man Kukulcan (Quetzalcoatl) set himself on fire for breaking his own rules, and as a result his ashes rose into space to form the planet Venus. Afterward, it was prophesied that his "divine energy" would return at the end of the historical age. Therefore, when the current Age of the Fourth Sun ends in 2012, the Mayas were predicting that Kukulcan/Venus (or higher consciousness) would descend upon the world. This is why they were keeping such a watchful eye on Venus, and calculating the exact date for the return of Kukulcan's Great Spirit.

In *The Dresden Codex*, the Mayas recorded the transit dates of Venus because they wanted future generations to know when his enlightening wisdom would return to Earth. They intended to share their knowledge with people who were living in 2012, and so, they left behind *The Dresden Codex* with its precise transit dates for

Venus. Below is the projected path for the next Venus transit on June 5-6, 2012, and where and when it will be seen from Earth.

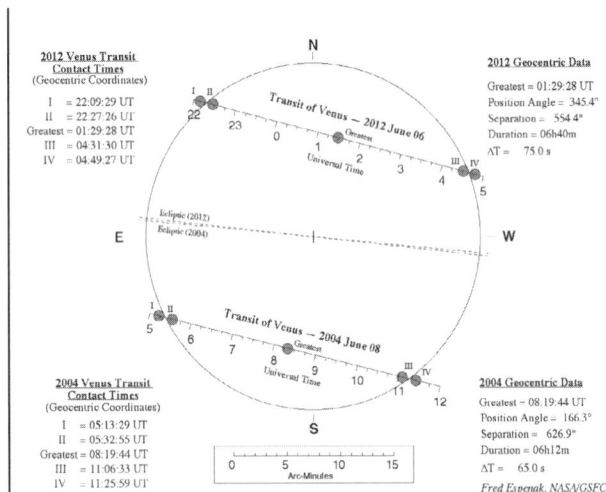

2012 Venus Transit Contact Times (Geocentric Coordinates)

I = 22:09:29 UT
II = 22:27:26 UT
Greatest = 01:29:28 UT
III = 04:31:30 UT
IV = 04:49:27 UT

2012 Geocentric Data

Greatest = 01:29:28 UT
Position Angle = 345.4°
Separation = 554.4"
Duration = 06h40m
ΔT = 75.0 s

Transit of Venus — 2012 June 06

Ecliptic (2012)
Ecliptic (2004)

Transit of Venus — 2004 June 08

2004 Venus Transit Contact Times (Geocentric Coordinates)

I = 05:13:29 UT
II = 05:32:55 UT
Greatest = 08:19:44 UT
III = 11:06:33 UT
IV = 11:25:59 UT

2004 Geocentric Data

Greatest = 08:19:44 UT
Position Angle = 166.3°
Separation = 626.9"
Duration = 06h12m
ΔT = 65.0 s

Fred Espenak, NASA/GSFC

Venus transit chart for 2004 & 2012

Additionally, a Venus-Pleiades conjunction will occur on June 27-28, 2012. During this time, the position of Earth, Venus, and the Pleiades will be in the same conjunction that was last seen in 813 CE (during the height of the Mayan empire). By using an astronomical software program, it is possible to recreate the Venus-Pleiades conjunction that appeared on March 13, 813 CE.

These coordinates from 813 CE will be very close to the upcoming 2012 Venus-Pleiades Conjunction. By the time Venus arrives in this position in June of 2012, it will be nearly 1200 years since its last appearance in this proximity. For those who believe in an approaching re-birth of spiritual energy in 2012, the Venus-Pleiades conjunction can be viewed as the metaphorical equivalent of "The Second Coming." Additionally, since Venus and the Pleiades were of great importance to the Mayas, the mystical interpretation of this event points to a merging of the higher and lower worlds.

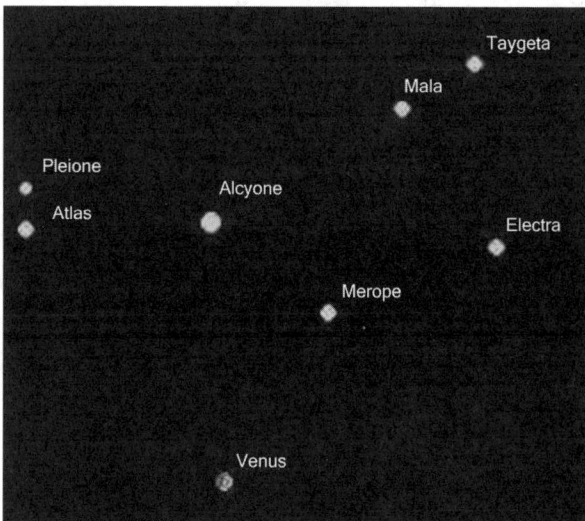

Venus and Pleiades

This archetypal vision is included in most religions as the day when Heaven and Earth are united as one.

Venus was symbolized by the five-pointed star because its path forms a pentagram over a period of 243 years. Therefore, the theme of "five" is an important construct in Mayan architecture and mathematics. According to Dr. Anthony Aveni of Colgate University:

> No one doubts that the Maya attributed "fiveness" to the changing aspect of Venus. In their inscriptions, we see it in the quincunx structure of the Venus-Lamat symbol, in the five pages of the Venus table, and the five sets of pictured intervals therein. In architecture, it appears in the arrangement of the Chac masks bearing Venus symbols that are stacked vertically in groups of five on the upper frieze of the Palace of the Governor at Uxmal or horizontally in the Nunnery at Chichen Itza (Sixth Palenque Round Table, 1986).

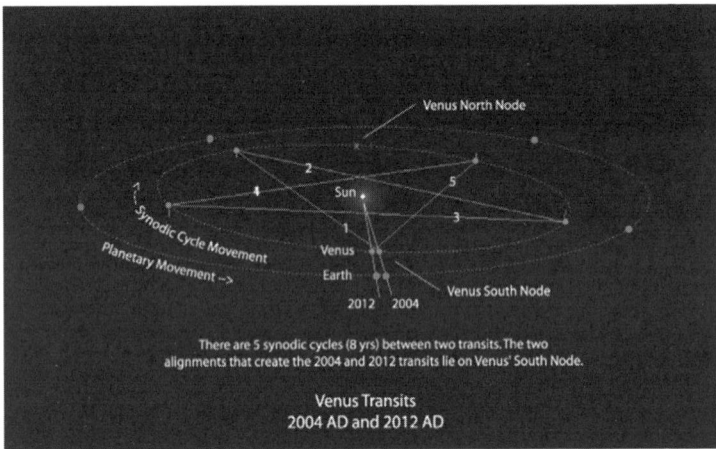

There are 5 synodic cycles (8 yrs) between two transits. The two alignments that create the 2004 and 2012 transits lie on Venus' South Node.

**Venus Transits
2004 AD and 2012 AD**

Venus Pentagram

Venus is also known as the "planet of love." She was the Roman goddess of love and the Greek love goddess, Aphrodite. It is important to understand that the pentagram originally represented the power of the Divine Feminine before it became known as the sign of the devil.

The Mayas did not attribute feminine qualities to Venus, however, the planet was still associated with love through their worship of Kukulcan as a *savior god*. According to legend, he was the manifestation of eternal love for his people, and he taught them the secrets of the Universe, the higher knowledge of the heavens, and the importance of love. It is not surprising that in Mayan mythology the loving god-man Kukulcan turns into the planet Venus. The important message for the ultimate meaning of 2012, therefore, is that the all-pervading Spirit of Kukulcan will return during the next transit of Venus, bringing a renewal of wisdom, compassion, and loving-kindness to the hearts and minds of people around the globe.

URBAN DESIGN

As Mayan cities spread throughout Mesoamerica, the importance of future site planning was minimal. Mayan architecture tended to integrate a great number of natural features, and their cities were built somewhat haphazardly. Some cities on the flat limestone plains of the northern Yucatan grew into great sprawling municipalities, while others, like Utzumacinta, used the natural loft of the topography to raise towers and temples to impressive heights.

The larger cities were more organized as the Mayas built urban centers to accommodate their growing populations. During the Classic Period, most urban designs were described as divisions of space between great monuments and causeways. The focus of urban design was finding a convenient location for open public plazas (Zocolos). The planning of interior space was of secondary importance. Only in the Late Post-Classic Period did the great Mayan cities develop into fortress-like defensive structures. This change was due to the emergence of new warring states that invaded the larger cities to obtain food, water, and valuables.

Typical Urban Complex

At the onset of large-scale construction during the Classic Era, a predetermined axis was typically established in a cardinal direction. Depending on the location of natural resources, such as freshwater wells (*cenotes*), the cities grew by using the causeways (*sacbe*). These roads connected the great plazas with numerous platforms, and consequently, an infrastructure was created for most Mayan cities.

At the heart of the Mayan city were large plazas surrounded by important government buildings and religious institutions. There were also great monuments, pyramid temples, and ball courts that were centrally located. Although city layouts evolved as nature dictated, careful attention was placed on the directional orientation of temples and observatories so that they were constructed in accordance with the orbits of the heavenly bodies. Outside the downtown area, there were homes for the lesser nobles, and smaller temples and individual shrines. In the outlying areas of the evolving urban core, there were modest homes for the lower classes.

Even though the Mayas were advanced in many ways, their cities were poorly constructed. Because they didn't have the large animals necessary for transporting heavy materials, metal tools, and pulleys, Mayan architecture required a tremendous amount of manpower. Therefore, the construction of government buildings, municipal centers, and general housing was of low quality. Additionally, the Mayas assigned their best craftsmen to work on the construction of pyramids and temples, which were their first priority.

The stones used for Mayan structures were taken from local quarries. Most often, the Mayas used limestone that was pliable, and could be shaped with stone tools. Their mortar consisted of crushed, burned, and mixed limestone that mimicked the properties of cement and was used for stucco finishing.

CEREMONIAL PLATFORMS

Ceremonial platforms were commonly made of limestone, as well, and were typically less than four meters in height. In these areas, the performance of public ceremonies, sacrifices, and religious rites took place, and they were constructed in the fashion of a foundation platform. They were often accented by carved figures, altars, and perhaps *tzompantli* (a stake used to display the heads of victims or defeated ball-game opponents).

Ceremonial Platform

BALL COURTS

There is much evidence of a certain ball game played by the Mayan men. The Olmecs are believed to be the creators of this game, however, many other Mesoamerican cultures played the ball game. The Mayas continued playing the ball game after the Olmecs disappeared, and many ball courts have been found at ancient sites, including Chichen Itza.

These ball courts were constructed on a grand scale throughout the Mayan empire. The typical architectural layout for a ball court included two high walls, an alley way, and end zones. They were enclosed on two sides by stepped ramps that led to ceremonial platforms or small temples, and they were a major part of the infrastructure of many cities. Both socially and politically, the ball courts represented the wealth and power of individuals at the highest levels of society.

Mayan Ball Court

The games were played with two teams, and the objective was to move the rubber ball into the opposing team's end zone without the use of their hands. They were allowed to use any other part of their bodies to move the ball forward. As the sport evolved, giant stone rings were installed on the walls of the alley way. These rings provided a difficult obstacle for scoring because the ball had to pass through the rings before going into the end zone.

The stakes were high for athletes participating in the ball games because they believed the gods would grant good fortune to the winning team. They also believed that the gods would give their crops the proper sunlight needed. However, if they lost, some of the worst players would be sacrificed, and the team would be disgraced.

The importance of the ball game to the Mayan people is evidenced in a reference to the game in the *Popol Vuh*, when speaking of a Creation myth about Hero Twins who were ball players. This

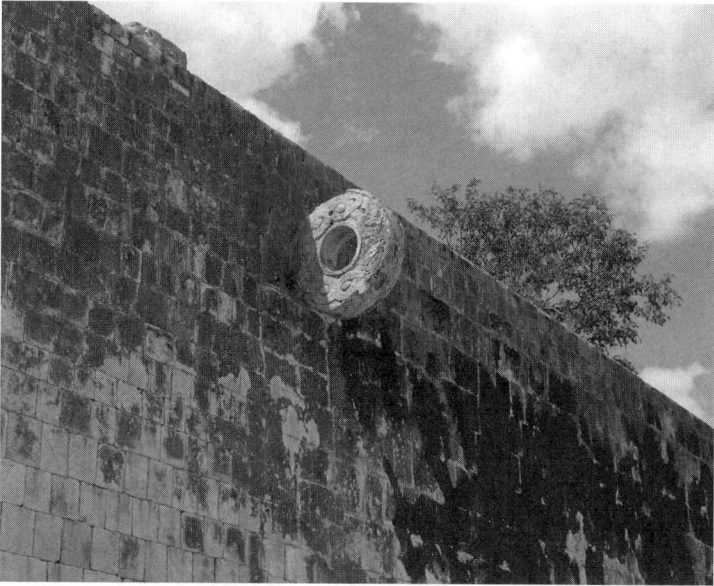

Wall of ball court showing ring (pelote)
through which ball had to pass

legend confirms the claim that the ball game was deeply implanted within Mayan culture.

The ball game continued to be played throughout Mesoamerica after most of the Mayas had disappeared. However, when the Spanish conquered Mesoamerica in 1519 CE, they brought an end to the ball game. Believing the game was a pagan ritual, they made it illegal.

PALACES

Palaces were often large with grand ornamentation. They were located close to the city's center, where the elite of the population were housed. Usually the palaces were only one-story tall and consisted of many small chambers and an interior courtyard. These structures had the functionality required of a residence, as well as the decorations required by those living there.

Mayan Palace Ruins

E-Groups

These complexes were structural configurations located at the center of most Mayan cities. They were oriented and aligned according to astronomical events such as the solstices and equinoxes. From an observation point on a nearby pyramid, the Maya could watch the sun rise behind the other buildings in the group. In this way, they could mark the summer and winter solstices (longest and shortest days of the year) as well as the vernal and autumnal equinoxes (when day and night are of equal length). These complex observatories were accompanied by iconographic art sculptures that tie astronomical observation into Mayan mythology. The structural complex is named for Group E at Uaxactun, which was the first found in Mesoamerica.

Photo of E-Group Structure

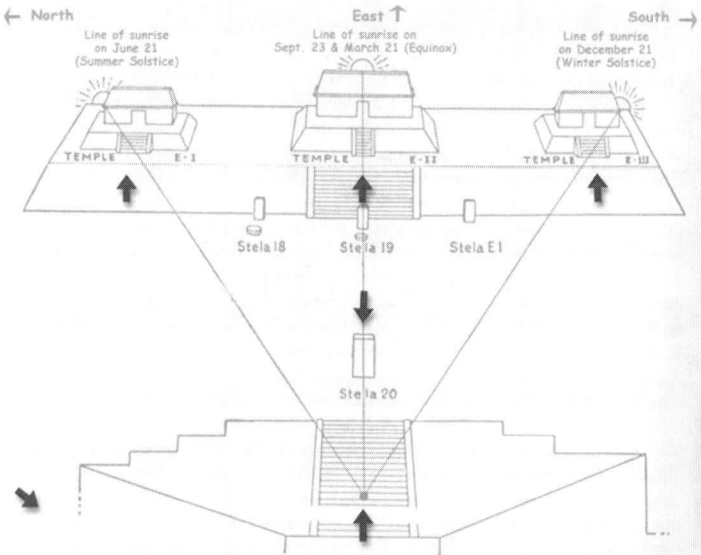

Diagram showing views across E Group Structures

Chapter 5

WHAT HAPPENED TO THE MAYAS?

With their awe-inspiring architecture and sophisticated concepts of astronomy and mathematics, the Mayas were undoubtedly among the world's great ancient civilizations. At the peak of their glory (c. 800 CE), the Mayan empire extended from Mexico's Yucatan Peninsula to Honduras. Then, almost in an instant, a society of some 15-22 million people imploded, leaving deserted cities, trade routes, and immense pyramids in ruins. Their sudden demise is one of the greatest mysteries of our time.

Art depicting Maya disappearance

There are only two plausible overarching reasons for Mayan depopulation and decline: non-ecological and ecological.

Non-ecological theories include:

+ overpopulation

+ foreign invasion

+ peasant revolt

+ collapse of key trade routes

Overpopulation: Some say overpopulation was the reason. However it is unlikely that overpopulation was the cause of the Mayan decline. If the population had been expanding, the builders of these great cities would have continued constructing new developments to house their people.

Foreign invasion: There is evidence of an invasion by an unknown group into the Yucatan. There is also speculation of a 9th century invasion from an army in the Gulf of Mexico lowland areas. It is possible that, as a result of this invasion, the Mayas of the Classic Period may have been annihilated. Some scholars point to the Toltecs as being responsible for this invasion. Conversely, other scholars believe that a military invasion cannot explain the complex and prolonged process of the collapse of the Mayas.

Peasant revolt: From 730-790 CE, there was great stress on peasants to build cities, ball courts, and other structures to show off the elite's influence and power. Without time to rest and with little compensation, the workers began to revolt.

Collapse of trade routes: The structure of their trading systems with large villages and other Mesoamerican civilizations began to deteriorate. Eventually, the vitally important trade route with Teotihuacan collapsed, but during the next 250 years, the Mayas created new trade routes in the lowland areas. Their primary trade consisted of obsidian, feathers, and cacao, while the lowlanders traded in flint, lime, pottery, slaves, and jaguar skins. The highlanders traded jade, cinnabar, and hematite (a red dye). However, trade route collapse might have been a temporary problem or could have occurred along with failure of the agricultural economy.

Some of the ecological problems that may have resulted in a sudden drop in the population include the following:

+ a major environmental disaster

+ a climate change

+ an epidemic-level disease

Major environmental disaster: Mayan cities were so expansive that they became vulnerable to environmental problems. They had many of the same challenges we have today due to infrastructure limitations within the environment. Additionally, they wasted their natural resources and did not have the technology for adapting to situations brought on by drought and natural disasters.

In 600 CE, the population of present-day southern Guatemala, Belize, and Northern Honduras (about 7,000 square miles) grew to over 12,000,000 people. With this dense population, the food supply could not be sustained with primitive farming methods during drought periods. By 910 CE, it is estimated that two-thirds of the Mayan population had disappeared.

Climate change: Research performed by scientists studying ancient pollen and lakebeds indicates that a drought was probably the major cause of the Mayan demise. Experts say the Mayas were particularly susceptible to long droughts because 95 percent of their population depended on lakes, ponds, rivers and reservoirs. Consequently, they needed to maintain an 18-month supply of water. Therefore, a drought lasting for an extended period of time would have deprived the people of adequate amounts of drinking water.

Epidemic-level disease: Along with the drought came disease in epidemic proportions, followed by lack of food and water. Additionally, it has been confirmed that the soil's production capacity had been exhausted. The theory that drought and disease were causes for the disappearance of the Mayas is postulated by researchers Dunn and Shimkin. They contend that, during the drought, the Mayas were suffering from endemic proportions of enteropathogens that caused dysentery and death. Other experts say that overuse of environmental resources would have disturbed the ecological equilibrium. This imbalance would have depleted nutrients and moisture in the soil. Additionally, with a lowering of the water table, there would have been an exploding population of parasitic and pathogen-carrying insects. Consequently, epidemic levels of parasites and disease would have been devastating to the Mayan population. With illnesses such as endemic dysentery, the mortality rate among children would have soared. Those who could survive these conditions would have become susceptible to other diseases later in life. Within a generation, there would have been a serious drop in the population. This deadly combination of disease and drought are the most likely factors to account for the disappearance of the Mayas.

According to a study published in an issue of *Science* (March 2003), a brutally dry climate that was punctuated by three intense droughts led to the end of the Mayan society. In this study, scientists analyzed the sediment core from the Carico Basin (near northern Venezuela), where archeological specimens were found. According to Gerald Haug, Professor of Geology at the University of Potsdam, "climate change is to blame for one of the most catastrophic collapses in human history." Swiss and U.S. researchers, seeking to identify the amount of rainfall during the Mayan decline, found that pristine sediment layers in the Carico Basin form distinct bands that correspond to dry and wet seasons.

According to scientists, there were three large mega-droughts, occurring between 810 and 910 CE. The timing of these droughts coincide with periodic downturns, as evidenced by the abandonment of cities and a decrease in building activity. The Mesoamerican climate can be likened to the American Dust Bowl during the Great Depression. Lasting for 220 years, these dry conditions were devastating to the entire region. As the climate began to change, the Mayas experienced starvation, thirst, and dire living conditions, and they rejected the idea that the gods were to blame for drought and famine. Desperate to obtain the necessities of life, the Mayan people turned to war. These were largely civil wars involving the starving villagers who were revolting against the priestly class and the elite. These revolutionaries blamed the priests and ruling class for the degenerating conditions of everyday life because the priests and elite were stealing expensive pieces of jade, art, gold, and jewels while the common people were dying of thirst and starvation. No longer could the villagers tolerate the oppressive rule and lavish lifestyle of their theocratic kings.

Warring Mayas

While these wars were occurring, the two superpowers of Tikal and Calakmul dominated the landscape. The wars between these two great city-states were some of the bloodiest and most violent in Mesoamerican history. These superpowers sought alliances with other cities in order to raid, conquer, and overthrow the royal elite of their enemies.

Interestingly, evidence was found in 2002 that revealed a plot by princes in Tikal to create their own empire. They planned this attack with the help of their alliances in nearby city-states. However, since the battle took place during the height of the drought season, the results were disastrous. Unfortunately, a number of pyramids and sacred temples were destroyed during this foray.

Another disastrous decision made during this war was the clearing of local trees for creating boundary fences as a form of defense. This action resulted in weeds invading the crops, ruining the harvest and causing further starvation. As the wars raged on, only the homeless and the ruins of the city remained. Eventually, the people fled the area, and the jungle reclaimed the territory that was once the great Mayan empire.

THE PRESENT

Today, there are very few people living in the region previously known as the Mayan empire. Many individuals find it difficult to believe that an advanced civilization once lived there. There are millions of Mayas still living in Mexico, Guatemala, and Honduras, while others have migrated to the United States. Miraculously, they were able to survive the arrival of the Spanish conquerors from Cuba, Hispaniola, and Spain, as well as the colonization of what is now Mexico. However, the culture of the modern-day Maya is very different from the world of their ancient ancestors. Many have been influenced by the merging of the pre-Columbians and the adoption of Christian beliefs, while others have not been affected by these outside influences.

In Post-Mayan villages in Guatemala, there are Catholic churches in the same places where local shamans hold chickens upside down while grasping eggs for purification rituals. These shamans wear white ceremonial robes of multicolored trim and use chickens to heal people during the mass. This melding of cultures is quite common in Post-Classic Mayan villages. Many Mayas have not lost their cultural identity, and their languages remain intact. For these people, Spanish is a second language used largely for the marketplace and church.

The author at a Mayan Temple, Palenque

Chapter 6

MAYAN RUINS

The ancient stone buildings in southern Mexico, Belize, Honduras and Guatemala are mesmerizing. However, most modern Mayas don't know very much about these buildings and simply refer to them by the generic *Xlappahk* ("old walls").The reason for the abandonment of these buildings, temples, and large structures is still being debated. The most recent analysis of Mayan glyphs is shedding light on the political in-fighting of state governments. This points to a complex, state-dominated social environment that eventually stopped building massive stone cities and became decentralized. Although the ancient Mayas had many notable achievements, it is the ruins that bring thousands of people each year to La Venta, Palenque, Bonampak, Yaxchilan, and Chichen Itza.

SOUTHERN CLASSIC RUINS

The Classic Period gave rise to many ornate and beautiful buildings such as those at Tikal, Copan, Quiriqua, Coba and Palenque. Each region has its own distinctive motif, and yet there are stylistic elements that are common to all. Classic Mayan sites typically consist of stepped platforms with masonry structures on top. These are often arranged around courtyards with very steep, stepped pyramids. Some pyramids were built with roof combs, which are high walls that extend upward. Additionally, carved panels have been found on interior walls and doorways.

The main temples at Tikal are characteristically Classic Mayan. There are similar temple pyramids throughout the Mayan region, but none are as tall as those in Tikal, which have 3,000 structures (or foundations) within about 6 square miles.

The Temple of the Inscriptions, Palenque, Mexico

At Palenque, another Classic site, the main pyramid is the Temple of the Inscriptions. It rises 75 feet above the plaza, but the back rests against a hill. The building of this type of pyramid would have required much less effort compared to the construction of a free standing pyramid.

Nohoch Mul Pyramid (Coba_Nohoch_Mul)

Coba, a site in Quintana Roo, Mexico, is a classic Mayan city. It was built around four large lakes, and the area has been continuously inhabited for a thousand years. The largest structure at the site, the Nohoch Mul (Great Mound) pyramid is 120 feet tall. One of more than 16 sacbes (manmade causeways) leads due west out of the city for 62.5 miles to the minor site of Yaxuna' and is the sacbe in Maya-land.

Puuc Style

In the low-lying hills of the Eastern Yucatan Peninsula, known as the Puuc, the Mayan buildings often exhibit a particular style named after the region. Built during the Late Classic Period, these structures define the style known as *Puuc*. The House of the Turtles at Uxmal is an exceptional example. The proportions of the building, along with the setting (overlooking the main quadrangle) and the unique turtle-motif, have led many to proclaim this building to be one of the finest in the region.

The upper third of all the walls are ornamented with inlaid building stones. The turtles at the top are depicted as walking horizontally on the wall, as seen in the photograph below.

House of the Turtles

Close up of one of the ornaments on the top portion, outside wall of the House of the Turtles, Uxmal, Yucatan, Mexico.

At the site of Sayil, approximately one-half mile from the main palace, is a small, ornate building recently cleared from the tropical scrub forest. The ornamentation—in the form of repeated columns—continues to the ground level. This design was achieved by affixing numerous carved stones on the exterior of the buildings and is a hallmark of the Puuc style.

Photo of doorway at Chicanna Campeche

Rio Bec or Chenes Style

In the Yucatan Peninsula, south of the Puuc hills, there is a distinct style of Mayan architecture known as Rio Bec or Chenes. For this mode of construction, (sometimes treated as two separate styles) ornamentation is the dominant factor.

In the bottom photo on the previous page is the monster doorway at Chicana, Campeche, Mexico. The doorway is the mouth of the monster. Although highly stylized, there are eyes above the door and a series of pendulant teeth hanging into the doorway. Nowhere else in the Mayan realm has ornamentation been taken to such extremes as in the regions of Rio Bec, Xupuhil, and Becan.

Furthermore, in this architectural approach, functionality has given way to effect. This can be seen in the many ruins which show that outer facades were built with no functionality. The stairs going up are impossible to climb, and the "buildings" at their summits are solid and have no rooms, indicating that the outer appearance of these quasi-pyramids was used to create the desired effect of inspiring awe and wonder among the people and nothing more.

Facade of the Codzpop Building, Kabah, 800-1200 A.D.

CHICHEN ITZA

In the Northern Yucatan, the city of Chichen Itza is a magnificent archeological site that is one the seven wonders of the Ancient World. *Chichen Itza* means "well of the Itza" in the Yucatec-Mayan language.

> It is believed among the Indians that with the Itzas who occupied Chichen Itza there reigned a great lord named Kukulcan, and that the principal building, which is called Kukulcan, shows this to be true [a reference to the Temple of Kukulcan or El Castillo]. They say that he arrived from the West. . . . They say that he was favorably disposed and had no wife or children and that . . . he was regarded in Mexico as one of their gods and called Quetzalcoatl: and they also considered him a god in Yucatan on account of his being a just statesman; and this was seen in the order which he imposed on Yucatan after the death of the lords [the overthrow of Maya rulers by the Itzas], in order to calm the dissension which their deaths had caused in the country (Diego de Landa Calderón, *Relacion de las Cosas de Yucatan*, c. 1566).

The stelae found at Chichen Itza depict battles that were waged between the invading Itzas and the Mayan residents. The Itzas were victorious and sacrificed any Mayas taken captive. John Spencer Carroll, in the epilog of his book *Quetzalcoatl*, notes,

> The Itzas had caused many of the lords of the land to be killed, and Kukulcan calmed the dissension that their deaths had caused. He ordered confessions and fasting, and he himself was celibate (J.C. Carroll, *A Search for Quetzalcoatl*, Santa Barbara, CA, 1994).

By 900 CE, the Southern Classic sites were abandoned or in decline. Monument construction from that period came to a stop. In the Northern Region, Chichen Itza continued to flourish until about 1200 CE. By this time, new construction at Chichen Itza ceased, and the city center fell into disuse. The site has remained an important pilgrimage destination to this day.

MAYAPAN

Mayapan translates as "the banner of the Mayas" (derived from the word *Maya* and the Nahuatl word *pantli*). *Chichen Itza* means "well of the Itza." The name of this new settlement symbolized a shift in Kukulcan's policy. According to Carroll:

> He abandoned Chichen Itza and founded the new capital of Mayapan. It was here, that he became king of all the factions in Yucatan. By choosing the name Mayapan, he conciliated both the indigenous Mayas and the foreign Itzas. Through negotiations, he induced the surviving lords of the land to settle at Mayapan, and he divided the land among them. He apportioned settlements "to each one according to the antiquity of his lineage and the worth of this person" (Carroll, 1994).

In 1002 CE, Kukulcan left Mayapan and returned to Champoton, where he stayed briefly before returning to the valley of Mexico. The new ruling family, the Cocoms established themselves as the rulers of Mayapan and the outer lying areas. "The League of Mayapan, created by Kukulcan and perpetuated by the Cocom family, endured almost five centuries and disintegrated finally in 1441 or 1446" (Carroll, 1994).

The city of Mayapan flourished between 1250 and 1450 CE and has several impressive features. There is a circular building that is unusual, and broken statues are scattered on the ground. It was one of a few walled Mayan cities that used walls as defensive structures. Mayapan was also the center of a large alliance of provinces. Demographic information indicates that the city was densely inhabited, with a population of 12,000 living within the 4 square kilometer area enclosed by the city walls.

TULUM

Not far from Mayapan, on the Quitana Roo Coast, there are the cities of Tulum and Tancah which date from the Post-Classic Period. Situated above the Caribbean on a limestone bluff, Tulum's site is quite spectacular. Also a walled city, Tulum had its own protected harbor and a small beach that provided seaward access. Although the buildings are of rougher construction than most Mayan sites, murals found in one of the temples are still visible and the original colors discernible. These murals display Toltec style figures with plants and animals.

TULA

Soon after the Mayas arrived in the valley of Mexico, they settled near high mountains and began construction of the city of Tula. It is located in a high area that was easily defended in the event of attack. Eventually, the local population (Toltecs) assimilated into the Mayan culture, and they were given advanced knowledge of the arts and sciences.

Myths concerning Tula were common in Mexican folklore. Among the first Europeans to mention this site was the Franciscan friar, Bernadino de Sahagun, who referred to it in his book, *A General History of the Things of New Spain* (also known as *The Florentine Codex*). According to de Sahagun, "Almost everything they [the Aztecs] accomplished—had been strongly influenced by peoples who inhabited central Mexico long before the Aztecs rose to power in the 14th century CE." These predecessors were the Mayans and the Toltecs.

Tula is about 50 miles to the north of Districto Federal, Mexico City, and can be described as "a little stepson" to earlier civilizations at Tenochtitlan and Teotihuacan. Not much information is available about Tula and the Toltecs because the site has been destroyed. However, there are still interesting statues that remain.

Toltec Statues at Tula

At the peak of the Tula civilization, it is estimated that a population of 60,000 lived within a 10-mile radius of the ceremonial center, and another 25,000 lived in the surrounding areas. From the layout of Tula, it can be observed that it had a civic center, ceremonial center, residential areas, and settlements that impacted urban development. Over the years, industrialization of Tula and agricultural technology resulted in extensive losses of archeological data. For those living in Tula, corn was an important crop requiring irrigation. In this high desert area, with an elevation of 7,000 feet, amaranth and maguey (cactus) were also grown. As with many of the smaller Mesoamerican cultures, there was a "farming only" zone from ½ mile wide up to 2 miles in length.

Tula had its earliest occupation with well-defined settlements from 400-200 BCE. The region was probably under the direct control of Teotihuacan because it was dependent on Tula for vast quantities of lime that were needed to build their pyramids. Different historical sources provide clues about the origins of the Toltecs. In 1519, Don Fernando wrote, "And the Toltecs...came to these parts, having first passed over great lands and seas, living in caves, and passing through great hardships until getting to this land" (*Primera Relacion*). Toltec laws were said to have been strict but justly enforced, and their most important priest-king was the famous Quetzalcoatl II. He was the "living divinity" who dwelled among the builders of Tulum.

Pyramids and Temples

Temples were huge structures that sat atop the towering Mayan pyramids; the closest place to the heavens. While recent discoveries point to the extensive use of pyramids as tombs, the temples rarely

Pyramid II in the Jungle, Tikal, Guatemala

contain burials. Residing atop the El Mirador pyramids at over 200 feet, the temples are impressive and decorated structures. The roof combs atop the temples were often carved with representations of rulers that could be seen from vast distances. Because they might have been the only structures that exceeded the height of the surrounding jungle, they may have been used as lookout towers for spotting enemy attacks.

OBSERVATORIES

The Mayas were avid astronomers and mapped out the orbits of celestial objects, such as the sun, the moon, Mars, and Venus. Aligning temples and pyramids with the occurrence of celestial events was another Mayan astronomical trait. They would observe the planets and stars from the top of round temples that are often described as "observatories" by modern tour-guides. However, many of these structures were dedicated to their god, Kukulcan, and the performance of religious rituals may have also taken place atop these temples.

THE MAYAN PYRAMIDS: HOW WERE THEY BUILT?

The ancient Mayans built two types of pyramids, those that were meant to be climbed and those that were not. The first type was used for sacrificial rituals, the other was held sacred. The steps built for these sacred structures were too steep to climb, and many times there were doorways leading to nowhere. During their rituals, the priests would climb the stairs of the pyramids from the ground to the top level, symbolizing the ascent from Earth to sky. The Mayans believed that when they climbed to the top of the pyramids, they would be closer to the gods.

Mayan pyramids also had other purposes. The pyramids extended upward, so their tops could be seen protruding out of the jungle. Consequently, they were used as landmarks, and they served as a reminder that the gods were ever present. Some pyramids housed burial chambers for high ranking officials. Inside these mammoth structures, narrow corridors led to small burial rooms which often contained treasures such as jade.

Pyramid Kukulcan

The materials used for building Mayan structures were normally types of stone found in the area surrounding the city. Limestone was plentiful in most Mayan settlements, and there were usually quarries close to the city where builders would obtain stones for construction. These stones were refined by chipping and flaking until their surfaces were flat.

The ancient Mayas did not use metal tools because metals were not found in the areas where they lived. Instead, they used simple methods, such as fire, and tools made of flint, obsidian, granite, limestone, and quartzite. These tools included basalt axes which provided precision for cutting and carving stone.

In order to judge vertical accuracy, the Mayas developed the "plumb bob", which was a heavy weight hung from a string or rope.

The Mayan architects did not build in right angles; instead, they used a measuring system known as *bilateral symmetry* (one half being the mirror image of the other).

Building Mayan pyramids and enormous monuments was a marvelous feat of engineering. This type of construction required a very large work force to haul the building materials since pulleys and wheels had not yet been invented in this part of the world. The workers had to carry loads of materials on their backs or roll them on logs to transport them to the construction site. While hundreds of peasants worked on the construction of a pyramid, the Mayas also had architects and king-priests to supervise the laborers.

Mayan Observatory

Often, the Mayas built one temple right on top of another, and several temples have been found underneath a single pyramid. Consequently, the pyramids became very large due to this method of construction. During the building process, the peasants constructed the platform, and the pyramids and palaces were built on top. Furthermore, when a new ruler came to power, the protocol was to add additional structures to the tops of buildings. In certain instances, a thorough remodeling could be expected. One of the largest temples in the ancient city of Tikal was continually built up over a period of 1,500 years. Pyramids and temples were usually found in the center of the city where lesser buildings were erected over time. The tops of the temples, pyramids and observatories provided an excellent vantage point from which to survey the city and decide where to construct new buildings.

The Mayan ruins offer astounding evidence of a sophisticated, dynamic Mesoamerican culture. Their monumental architectural achievements provide proof of their overall innovative genius. When the Spanish arrived in the New World in the 16th century, they were stunned by the astonishing beauty of the Aztec capitol of Tenochtitlan (part of Mexico City). Their engineering achievements rival the magnificent architecture of Venice and other great cities of Europe. Later on, when the Spanish explored the continent, they found abandoned Mayan cities that were even more impressive.

Chapter 7

ASTRONOMICAL AGES

The Mayas and Aztecs had a well developed system of cosmology called the *Long Count Calendar*. It is based on a unit of time called a *baktun*, which is a 394 year cycle ruled by one of their major gods. According to the Mayan elders, the current World of the Fourth Sun will end on the winter solstice of 2012 and the new World of the Fifth Sun will begin at that time.

Tzolkin calendar combines 13 numbers and 20-day signs for a 260 day sacred calendar

Each baktun is ruled by a new god, and each god is often referred to by the Aztec name since we don't know all the names of the Mayan gods. The Fourth World comprises 13 baktuns, and the Mayas believed that each baktun was associated with gods of the day and gods of the night. Moreover, scholars agree that most civilizations follow cycles of light and darkness. These cycles become evident in such areas as religion, language, writing, calendars, and communication.

By moving backward in time, we can say that the Mother Goddess was at the height of her power and there was a balance established between the divine masculine and feminine. The domestication of plants and animals was spreading from the mountains to the fertile river valleys, and hunter-gatherers were evolving into farmers. Archeological evidence from before 3114 BCE indicates that people were engaging in hunting, plowing, farming, and making artistic objects.

Baktun 5 started in 1140 BCE and came under the Aztec god of death. During this time, the major Olmec city of San Lorenzo was deserted, followed by the birth of a new central city called *La Venta*. Baktun 6 started about 748 BCE under *Cinteotl*, the Aztec god of maize and sustenance. Unfortunately, there is very little historical evidence available to describe baktuns 7 and 8. Baktun 9 lasted from 435 to 830 CE, when the Classic Mayan Age began its decline. In this period, the great cities of Copan and Palenque were deserted, and Teotihuacan collapsed. Subsequently, baktun 10 came under the Aztec goddess of birth, *Yohudlicitl*, who guided the

Aztec Sun Disk, Aztec calendar, Museo de Antropologia - D.F. – Mexico

Mayas to Chichen Itza after 830 CE. In this location, they built the famous Kukulcan Pyramid Temple (El Castillo), where the Feathered Serpent's shadow climbs up the pyramid (step-by-step) during the spring and fall equinoxes. Baktun 11 started under the Aztec god, *Before Dawn*, in 1224 CE, which was another dark age. Baktun 12 began in 1618 CE under the Aztec god, *Ometeotl*, the dual creator god who introduced the present era. Since then, humanity has been experiencing an age of accelerating advances in science, technology, exploration, and transportation.

Pictured opposite is the Aztec Sun Disk, which weighs about 25 tons and is about 12 feet in diameter and 3 feet deep. At the top, there are two massive serpents coming down out of the heavens and onto the Earth. As the Sun and Fire gods come down in the form of serpents, their heads are changed from serpent to human.

A more popular replica of The Sun Disk

The Sun Disk has a circle in the middle with the Sun god's face. Above the face is a pyramid, with four squares surrounding the center circle. Each one of these squares represents one of the ancient ages. The circle in the middle is the current time period we are living in: the Age of Movement or Change. Thus, there are only five ages shown here.

Some people begin their interpretation of the ancient ages with the first square to the left of the pyramid and move around the circle counterclockwise. Others begin with the square on the right of the pyramid, then move to the one on the left, and continue moving in this direction. Interestingly, if we begin with the square on the right of the pyramid and move counterclockwise, the ages correspond to the mythologies of the Egyptians and other ancient cultures.

The first square, the Jaguar Sun or the Age of the Jaguar, has a stylized jaguar in it. In the mythology of this age, the people were powerful and sophisticated, but were not incarnate beings in the sense of physical form. They were compared to spirits, angels, or Egyptian "godlings" that consist of energy and spirit.

Moving to the next square, we come to the Age of Water or the Age of the Fish. This myth speaks of the children of God who descended from the heavens and lost their way. They couldn't see the horizon and didn't know where they were going. Suddenly, the great god Quetzalcoatl (the Feathered Serpent) descended from above and created a firmament so that the children could reach their earthly destination.

In the next age, the Age of Fire, there was an attempt to make physical bodies for the children of God. These were known as blue maize or corn body. As the story unfolds, the blue maize people were perfect and made it possible for the spirits to incarnate. However, the children were still weak of mind and had jealous feelings and vices, and once again they lost their way. Subsequently, this age came to an end after volcanic explosions and meteors from heaven hit the Earth. Some believe that this disturbance resulted in the destruction of Plato's Atlantis.

The Fourth age is called the Age of Wind and is symbolized in the fourth square with a depiction of a stylized turkey. The children of God were like turkeys and were unable to fly or move away from Earth. They became possessed by the world and were ensnared in the evolution of matter. Then, the children of God began incarnating on Earth and became trapped in the Cycle of Rebirth.

The cycle of the Fifth age is known as the Age of Change. Accordingly, the world is transforming from a heavy, dense materialistic condition to a spiritually liberating one. According to legend, the era to follow is the Age of the Spirit of All Living Things. It will be a time when the inner essence of collective humanity will regain its natural sense of energy and spiritual resonance. Once this vital spark of life is renewed within the human condition, each individual will begin to awaken to the Spirit of All Living Things.

ASTRONOMICAL PRECISION

The primary resources for understanding Mayan astronomy are the epigraphic records in four Mayan codices: the Dresden, Madrid, Paris, and the controversial Grolier. Fortunately, these hieroglyphic writings survived the Spanish book burnings of the Conquest Period. The rediscovery of these volumes in European libraries in the mid-19th century marked the beginning of modern inquiry into the intellectual achievements of the Mayas.

Post-Conquest writings depict calendar cycles, and numbers play an important role in deciphering Mayan script. In particular, the work of Diego de Landa presents Mayan calendar glyphs. Landa reports two types of months noted in the Yucatan and notes that lunar months began with the appearance of a new moon. Landa also reports that the New Year began on 12 Kan 1 Pop in 1553 (Vincent H. Malström, "Edzna: Earliest Astronomical Center of the Maya?" *Arqueoastronomía y etnoastronomía en Mesoamérica*, 1991).

This correlation later proved useful in aligning Mayan and modern calendars.

The Pyramid of the Sun in Teotihuacan

During the 19th century, Abbe Brasseur de Bourbourg recognized the day-glyphs after discovering de Landa's *Relacion de las Cosas de Yucatan*. Landa provides drawings with the names of corresponding months and presents four glyphs that fall on the first day of each month. He also provides a calendar that aligns European months with the Native Calendar and includes names of calendar cycles and other hieroglyphic symbols relating to European alphabetic signs (Cázares Leon and Maria del Carmen, *Fray Diego de Landa, Relacion de las Cosas de Yucatan*. Mexico City: Consejo Nacional para la Cultura y las Artes, 1994). Consequently, this discovery allowed scholars to decode a sequence for reading the glyphs and for deciphering the Long Count notation. Brasseur de Bourbourg also identified the sun or kin glyph, which he associates with the day.

Furthermore, Ernst Förstemann identifies the Venus glyph on the basis of its recurrence in the Venus Table of the *Dresden Codex*. Förstemann notes the sum of a row of numbers totals 584, which corresponds to the Venus cycle. This includes labeling Venus as the morning star and observing its dual role as the evening star with an inferior solar conjunction (*Commentary on the Maya Manuscript in the Royal Public Library of Dresden. Harvard University, Peabody Museum, Papers,* Vol. IV, No. 2, Cambridge: Peabody Museum, 1906). In addition, Förstemann recognized the eclipse intervals of 177 days and 146 days. In 1895, Förstemann made a valuable contribution by identifying the celestial bands in the codices as a distinct type of hieroglyphic composition representing cosmic entities. He was the first to identify the celestial band hieroglyphs in the *Dresden Codex* (Beth A. Collea, *The Celestial Bands in Maya Hieroglyphic Writing, Archaeoastronomy in the Americas,* Los Altos, CA: Ballena Press & Center for Archaeoastronomy, 1981).

According to this study, it is widely accepted that the ancient civilizations of Mesoamerica had an advanced astronomical knowledge that was comparable to their contemporaries in other parts of the world. These discoveries were made by using fundamentals that underlie the practices of astronomy, numeration, and calendrics.

THE MAYAN 5,125 YEAR SHIFT

As previously stated, the Mayan grand cycle of 13 baktuns—or 5,125 years—began in 3114 BCE and will end in 2012 CE. The Tzolk'in or Short Count Calendar is a 260-day calendar based on the nine-month cycle of human gestation. This calendar was used to determine personality traits and time harmonics similar to Western astrology.

In order to understand why certain writers believe that the Mayan Long Count Calendar ends in 2012, it is necessary to review certain astrological and galactic cycles. These cycles were intended to explain long periods of time for future humanity and how different intensities of light affect the Earth as it travels through the Milky Way. The cycles of the sun and Venus are significant light cycles, and eclipses seen from Earth are considered fundamental cycles of dark-ness. This interrelationship between cycles of light and dark reveals an evolutionary path of life and consciousness within the galaxy.

Chapter 8

GALACTIC ALIGNMENT

A so-called "galactic alignment" occurs when the sun is moving along the "galactic equator" of the Milky Way, and the Earth and galactic center are lined up during the winter solstice. Supposedly, this event occurs only once every 25,920 years, when the Precession of the Equinoxes comes to an end. This precession occurs as a result of the Earth's slow wobbling on its axis, making it appear as though the constellations are shifting one degree every 72 years. Therefore, 72 years X 360 degrees (the full circle of the precessional cycle) = 25,920 years for *viewing* the 12 constellations *as they appear* to pass overhead in the nighttime sky.

Planet Earth

According to popular books on 2012, a "local" galactic alignment between Earth, the sun's horizon, and the center of the Milky Way occurs every year on the winter solstice. The "long distance" galactic alignment refers to the sun's crossing of the galactic equator of the Milky Way as it aligns with the center of the galaxy and Earth.

Before questioning the validity of the "2012 Galactic Alignment", it is important to understand the claims being made by writers and "experts" on the 2012 lecture circuit. Following is an encapsulated version of their galactic alignment theory:

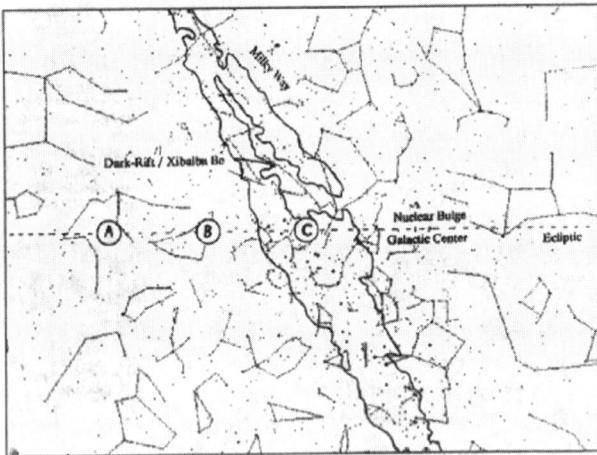

Winter Solstice Sun in the Milky Way

Point A is the approximate location of the December solstice sun within the Milky Way in 1000 BCE; Point B represents the sun's location in 500 CE; and point C is where the sun will be on 12/21/2012. On this day, as the Mayan Long Count Calendar comes to an end, the sun will be at the center line of the Milky Way (the galactic equator). Furthermore, this alignment is supposed to occur at the "nuclear bulge" of the galactic center.

Galactic Alignment 99

Nick Fiorenza developed an illustration of the precession of the equinoxes that purportedly progresses in tandem with the galactic alignment. Additionally, predictions about this event include references to "the solstice-galaxy alignment" and the "Holy Cross" of the equinox axis in the "dark rift" of the Milky Way. Interestingly, there are others who believe that the "solstice-galaxy alignment" and "equinox-galaxy cross" are simply one and the same.

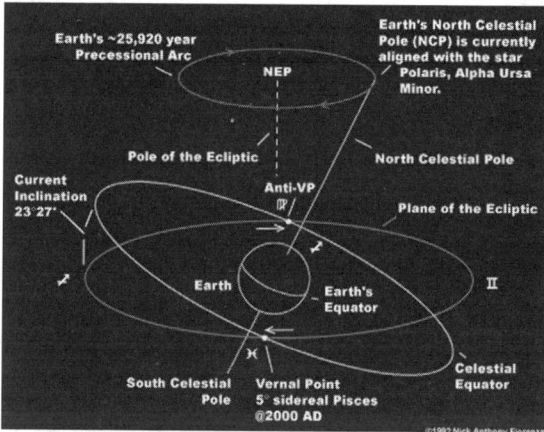

Fiorenza's illustration of the precession of the equinoxes

Circular view from the Sun looking at the Milky Way

Location of sun on a spiral band (NASA)

However, the view from Earth when watching the sun's path is nothing more than an illusion (due to the wobble of the Earth). The constellations are not moving either. Thus, the precession of the equinoxes is an illusion, as well.

Therefore, there will be no galactic alignment in 2012 because the sun and Earth are not going to be in alignment with either the galactic equator or the center of the Milky Way (the galactic center). In fact, according to astrophysicists, the galactic equator is not a separate object and is not easily detected from natural evidence in the area around the equator. As a comparison, if you were trying to find the Earth's equator, you wouldn't find that black circular band that appeared on the globe you used in school. This black band was just a circular marker designed to help you find the middle of the Earth. When the black band is no longer there, you will find it is extremely difficult to pinpoint the exact areas that are above and below the equator. Therefore, trying to locate the precise position of the Earth's equator is extremely difficult when using the naked eye.

Likewise, it is not easy to find the equator of the Milky Way, and there is no astronomical benefit to the Earth by crossing the galactic equator or being above or below it.

Our Solar System is situated 28,000 light years from the galactic center of the Milky Way in the outer regions of the galaxy. It is located well within the disk of the galaxy and approximately 20 light-years (117 billion miles) above the equatorial plane. According to scientists, the sun will be entering the galactic equator in 30 million years, and *depending on one's view from outer space*, there will be an equatorial alignment between the sun, Earth, and the galactic center. As far as we know, the sun has always been inside the disk of the Milky Way. It has crossed the galactic equator many times in the past, and there is no record of any cosmic event occurring as a result of this crossing.

So, where will our Solar System be in relation to the galactic center on December 21, 2012? Science tells us that our Solar System is revolving around the center of the galaxy every 225 million years. While doing so, it is moving up and down as it travels across the galactic equator every 33 million years. At the present time, the sun is north of the galactic equator and there is evidence that it crossed this plane over 3 million years ago. Therefore, the Solar System continues to move away from the galactic plane and will not cross it again for another 30 million years.

To confirm the fact that a galactic alignment *will not* occur in 2012, Mayan scholar Vincent H. Malström (Professor Emeritus, Dartmouth College) offers his insights on this subject:

> According to [a best-selling author], the Maya fixed the termination of their Long Count to mark the coincidence of the winter solstice with the "galactic center of the universe."... In helping him reach this conclusion, [the author] gratefully acknowledges the "boost of clarity and insight" which he received from reading Edmonson's work.... He assures us furthermore that it was a

relatively simple matter for the Maya to identify the galactic center of the universe because it lies in the middle of the Milky Way,
which they visualized as "the birth canal of the Mother Goddess",
"a source-point or creation place." What this has to do with the
winter solstice, or how the latter, which can be easily marked by
horizon-based astronomy during the day, can be shown to coincide with the center of the Milky Way, which can only be seen at
night, he doesn't inform us. At least unlike Thompson, who put
down the Maya as mere "astrologers" rather than "astronomers,"
our brash new savant has credited a people who had no knowledge that the Earth was even round, much less that it wobbled
on its axis, with more than supernatural powers. In the process,
however, it would seem that [this author] has advanced our
understanding of the Maya from the sublime to the ridiculous.

But, before rejecting this imaginative hypothesis altogether,
I decided to test it to see if, in fact, the Maya themselves would
have been able to view this momentous "event" as it takes place
on December 21, 2012. For this purpose, I used the Voyager
computer program as my "planetarium" and I chose the Mayas'
major astronomical center of Edzná in the Yucatán as my viewing point. (Actually, it makes no difference which viewing point
is selected within the Maya realm, for the results are the same
everywhere in Mesoamerica.) As dawn approaches on that critical day, the Galactic Center, imbedded as it is in the Milky Way,
would "appear" above the horizon just as the sun itself does about
6 degrees farther to the North. Of course, the only problem is
that, with the Milky Way gone as a point of reference, the Galactic Center is also invisible, and it remains so as long as the sun is
above the horizon. Expectantly I looked forward to the sunset,
hoping to regain my critical reference point once the sky again
darkened. But no such luck. I found that the Galactic Center
slipped below the horizon at 4:57 pm that afternoon, exactly half

an hour before the sun itself sets some seven degrees farther to the south. So much for "much ado about nothing" (*The Astronomical Insignificance of Maya Date 13.0.0.0.0*, 2003).

There is another troubling issue concerning the galactic alignment theory. It uses the Egyptian Zodiac as a 26,000 year measuring device instead of the Mayan Zodiac's precessional cycle (which is still not completely understood). Today, some contemporary authors have borrowed the 26,000 year cycle from the Egyptians and have taken license to combine it with the sun's position at the end of the Mayan age in 2012. Therefore, unless the Egyptians were able to share their astronomical information with the Mayans, there can be no basis for claiming that the Egyptian and Mayan Zodiacs are connected. There is an additional claim that on 12/21/12 the sun will find itself on a "cosmic cross" when its path (the ecliptic) intersects with the equator of the Milky Way. For many people, this imaginative idea could be construed as a "crucifixion of the sun" on a "cosmic cross" that leads to its re-birth through a "birth canal" or

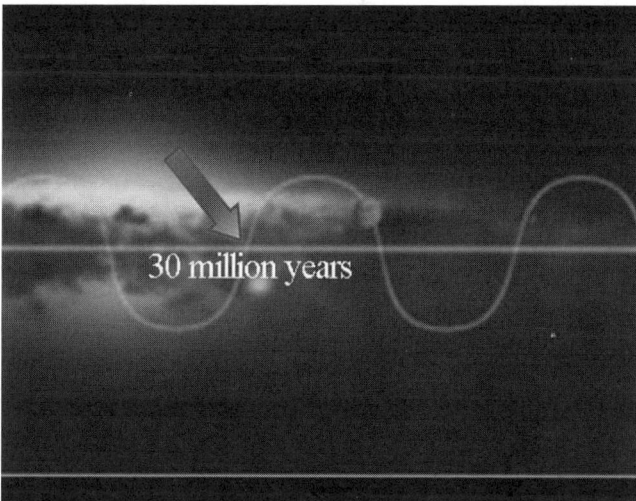

30 million years

Sun's orbit around the Galactic Equator

"dark rift" in the galaxy. As previously noted, this event does occur every 33 million years. However, the sun was in this position 3 million years ago and isn't due to return for another 30 million years. Therefore, the sun will not be positioned on a cosmic cross in 2012.

Here we find an attempt to exploit the symbolic metaphor of "crucifixion and resurrection" as a transit-point for entering a new world age. This deceptively clever idea corresponds to the star of Bethlehem positioned over the manger, which was to become the starting point for the Gregorian Calendar in 1582 CE.

Also, coinciding with the year 1 CE was the beginning of the astronomical Age of Pisces. Therefore, it is obvious that certain "2012 pundits" are falsely creating a "crucifixion of the sun" to correspond with the Biblical theme of Messianic consciousness coming into the world in both the years 1 and 2012. It is an intriguing concept that may sell books and movie tickets, but there is not one shred of truth in this fantastical scenario.

Unfortunately, there will be a great number of people who will correlate the crucifixion-resurrection theme of the Bible to the galactic alignment's motif of the sun's being reborn in the "dark rift" of the Milky Way. It is safe to say that the galactic alignment is a 21st century, Westernized conglomeration of half-truths lacking any basis in scholarship, history, or science. According to NASA senior scientist David Morrison:

> There is no alignment with the center of the galaxy in 2012 or anytime...one simple test is to ask if any of these claims are made by real scientists, or if they are being reported in the [media]. These stories about alignments or disasters striking in 2012 do not pass this test.

As for predicting an exact date for a galactic alignment, Frasier Cain explains why it is extremely difficult to do so:

When is the galactic alignment going to happen? It's almost impossible to know exactly. The Milky Way is 100,000 light-years across, but only 1,000 light-years thick. So, during the course of that 64 million year cycle, the Sun rises above the galactic plane 500 light-years, passes down through the galactic plane, until it's 500 light-years below and then comes back up again… it's just like crossing an imaginary line in space, like traveling from Canada to the United States in your car (*Universe Today*, 2009).

While December 21, 2012, is still a critical end date for the Mayan Long Count Calendar, it is clear that the sun's location on this day will have absolutely nothing to do with the ultimate meaning of 2012.

Destruction of the Earth

Chapter 9

HOW MANY WAYS CAN OUR EARTH BE DESTROYED?

Many people believe that the world is coming to an end in 2012. However, this type of speculation is nothing new. Individuals throughout history have made predictions about the world ending on a specific date. So far, none of them have been right.

For those in the West, *The Book of Revelation* has been a constant reminder that the world will be destroyed by fire. This concept of "end of days" has been part of Western culture since 325 CE (when the New Testament became the Christian Bible). Consequently, a number of religious groups over the last 1,000 years have predicted that Armageddon would arrive during their lifetimes.

Why do well-known individuals continue to predict an end-of-times? The answer is simple: there's a lot of money to be made by doing so. Also, this type of doomsday scenario attracts much attention by frightening others and attempting to control them. It's a self-serving, terrifying phenomenon; and over the last millennium, dozens of unsubstantiated, random, and misguided theories have caused serious psychological damage to millions of innocent people:

> 1000 CE - Jan 1: Many Christians in Europe had predicted the end of the world on this date. As the date approached, Christian armies waged war against some of the pagan countries in Northern Europe. Christ was supposed to return in the year 1000 (Rev. 20: "But the rest of the dead lived not again until the thousand years were finished. This is the first resurrection"). Meanwhile, many Christians had given their possessions to the

Church in anticipation of the end in the year 1000 CE. When Jesus did not appear, the Church did not return the gifts.

1033: Some believed this to be the 1000th anniversary of the death and resurrection of Jesus. His second coming was anticipated.

1147: Gerard of Poehide decided that the millennium had actually started in 306 CE during Constantine's reign. Thus, the end of the world was expected in 1306 CE.

1179: John of Toledo predicted the end of the world during 1186. This estimate was based on the alignment of the planets.

1205: Joachim of Fiore predicted in 1190 that the Antichrist was already in the world, and that King Richard of England would defeat him. The millennium would then begin, sometime before 1205.

1284: Pope Innocent III computed this date by adding 666 years onto the date that Islam was founded.

1346 and later: The black plague spread across Europe, killing one third of the population. This was seen as the prelude to an immediate end of the world. Unfortunately, the Christians had previously killed many of the cats, fearing that they might be friendly to witches. So, by killing cats, there were more rats, and it was the rat fleas that spread the black plague.

1496: This was approximately 1500 years after the birth of Jesus. Some mystics in the 15th century predicted that the millennium would begin during this year.

1524: Many astrologers predicted the imminent end of the world due to a worldwide flood. They obviously had not read the Genesis story of the rainbow.

1533: Melchior Hoffman predicted that Jesus was returning a millennium and a half after the nominal date of his execution, in 1533. The New Jerusalem was expected to be established in Strasbourg, Germany. Hoffman was arrested and died in a Strasbourg jail.

1669: The Old Believers in Russia believed that the end of the world would occur in this year. Twenty thousand burned themselves to death between 1669 and 1690 to protect themselves from the Antichrist.

1689: Benjamin Keach, a 17th century Baptist, predicted the end of the world for this year.

1736: British theologian and mathematician William Whitson predicted a great flood similar to Noah's for Oct. 13 of this year.

1792: This was the date of the end of the world calculated by some believers in the Shaker movement.

1794: Charles Wesley, one of the founders of Methodism, thought Doomsday would be in this year.

1830: Margaret McDonald, a Christian prophetess, predicted that Robert Owen would be the Antichrist. Owen helped found New Harmony, Indiana.

1843: The Millerites, lead by farmer John Miller, preached to thousands that the end was coming based on biblical calculations. After the world didn't end, this movement eventually became known as Jehovah's Witnesses.

1874: The Second Adventists (affiliated with Nelson H. Barbour) agreed with other Adventist groups that the "last days" had started in 1799 and would end in 1874.

1891: Joseph Smith, founder of the Mormon Church, said he spoke to God and was told that the Second Coming would occur over the next 56 years, which was to be followed by the end-of-days.

1982: Pat Robertson told the TV audience of the 700 Club that he knew when the world would end. Robertson said, "I guarantee you by the end of 1982 there is going to be a judgment on the world" (religioustolerance.org).

For those who want to believe that a catastrophic event is coming in 2012, there are quite a few disaster theories to choose from. In fact, the internet is filled with information on just about every conceivable way that Earth can be destroyed. Fortunately, there is no scientific proof to support any of these doomsday scenarios; but, this hasn't stopped modern-day prophets from offering their mindless prattle. Here are just a few examples of forecasted cosmic anomalies that are intended to frighten people until December 21, 2012.

FIERCE GAMMA RAYS FROM THE BLACK HOLE

Like most big galaxies, the Milky Way hosts a super-sized black hole at its center. Nothing, not even light, can escape its strong gravitational force. Cosmic material swirls towards this black hole from as far away as a few million light-years, and it is the power source for the entire galaxy.

The Space Research Institute in Moscow and the Max Planck Institute for Astrophysics in Germany indicate that in other galaxies, it is common to find black holes 100 million times brighter than those in our galaxy. According to these research institutes, it has been demonstrated that our black hole was a million times brighter only 350 years ago.

The variation in brightness is related to the amount of matter being absorbed into the black hole as fuel. It is estimated that every second, 10 trillion tons of gases and space dust are being devoured by

Black Hole

the black hole. Based on past history, the amount of fuel available for the black hole will increase; however, there is no way to predict when this process will begin again. Even if a large flare-up from the center of the Milky Way occurs, it will pose no threat to life on Earth. Fortunately, the planet's magnetosphere protects us from most gamma rays, and the ozone layer protects us from the sun's harmful radiation. The molecules in the atmosphere absorb high energy photons preventing gamma rays from reaching us on the ground.

So, is there any evidence to back up the claim that Earth will be destroyed by gamma rays from the black hole in 2012? No. There is no evidence whatsoever. As far as anyone can tell, there will be nothing extraordinary happening in the cosmos in December, 2012.

Milky Way

Then why are the doomsayers so worried about the Milky Way's black hole lashing out gamma rays and destroying the Earth? The BBC asks the same question:

> What effect will this giant black hole 28,000 light years away have on us and the rest of the galaxy around it? These are questions that have been puzzling astronomers for the last few years—and in June [2000], two separate groups of scientists found evidence that points to a startling answer. Rather than being destructive parasites, it seems that super-massive black holes may be essential in the very creation of the galaxies they live in ("Supermassive Black Holes," *BBC Horizon*, 2000).

However, all is not lost for the doomsayers. They can still look forward to the day—3 billion years from now—when the black hole in the center of our Milky Way galaxy will probably destroy our Earth. In January 2000, physicist John Dubinski graphically described the fate of our galaxy: "In 3 billion years we will collide with the next door galaxy, Andromeda. The resulting apocalypse will force our Solar System and Earth out of orbit" ("Supermassive

Black Holes," 2000). Dubinski says there is a 50-50 chance that the Earth will hurtle toward the black hole at that time.

A COSMIC JOLT CAUSES A POLE SHIFT

Theoretically, a pole shift occurs when the Earth shifts on its axis, thus causing the North and South Poles to move as much as 40 degrees from their current locations. Hugh Auchinloss Brown, a distinguished author and electrical engineer, proposed a catastrophic pole shift. He based his hypothesis on the notion that ice at the poles causes a cyclical tipping of Earth on its axis about once every 7 thousand years.

Another well-known supporter of pole shift theory is Charles Hapgood. In his books, *The Earth's Shifting Crust* (Museum Press, 1958) and *The Path of the Pole* (Philadelphia: Chilton, 1970), Hapgood contends that the accumulation of ice at one or both poles can interrupt the Earth's rotational balance and cause the outer crust to

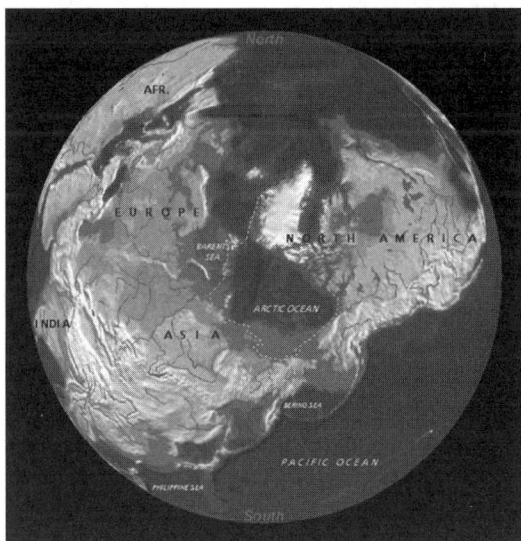

Placement of continents if Earth were to experience a pole shift

slip around the core. Hapgood states that it takes about five thousand years for a shift to occur, with intervals of 20 to 30 thousand years between shifts. In addition, Hapgood asserts that the movement of the poles is confined to within 40 degrees. He believes that the location of the North Pole has varied among the Yukon Territory, Hudson Bay, and a spot in the Atlantic Ocean between Iceland and Norway.

Hapgood's theory is an example of a slow pole shift which does not cause massive destruction. However, there are other theories proposing that a sudden shifting of the poles would cause immediate devastation from earthquakes and tsunamis.

Whether slow or sudden, a pole shift would result in major climate changes across the Earth. Accordingly, there would be significant temperature changes in all regions of the globe.

Other theories accounting for pole shift include the following possibilities:

+ an asteroid or comet hitting the Earth at an angle would cause the crust and upper mantle (the lithosphere) to move separately from the underlying asthenosphere on which they rest, resulting in the Earth's shifting on its axis.

+ a highly magnetic object from space passing closely enough to affect the Earth's magnetic field would cause the lithosphere to reorient temporarily until the sun's magnetic field was once again stronger than that of the intruding object.

+ an avalanche or other natural phenomena would cause a redistribution of the mass of the Earth, resulting in mantle shift.

Obviously, such a dramatic physical pole shift as suggested by the three preceding scenarios would need to be caused by a sudden event of tremendous energy. Increase of solar energy alone would not be enough to cause such a catastrophic event. While there have been a few degrees of pole shift during the Earth's history, the shifting of a few degrees would not constitute a complete pole reversal. According to oceanographers William W. Sager (Texas A&M University) and Anthony A. P. Koppers (Scripps Institution of Oceanography), the "data set indicates that a polar shift took place at a rate of between 5 and 10 degrees per million years." Sager explained that in geological time, a pole shift happens "within the blink of an eye" ("Texas A&M Oceanographer Challenges Plate Tectonics as Reason for Poles' Shift," *Science News*, 25 Jan. 2000). If a *fast* polar shift takes millions of years to occur, then it is not possible to predict a specific date that would coincide with the end of the Mayan calendar. Therefore, such a prediction entails only guesswork.

Additionally, some "experts" are claiming that the rotation of the Earth will abruptly stop in 2012, and start spinning in the opposite direction. However, there is no scientific data to support this theory. (Why would the Earth suddenly "decide" to shift into reverse anyway?) This idea should not be confused with the theory of geomagnetic reversal, which refers to a polar change in magnetic orientation. Let's take a closer look at this phenomenon.

REVERSAL OF EARTH'S GEOMAGNETIC FIELD

Geomagnetic reversal is a shift of the *magnetic* poles rather than the physical poles. Like physical pole shifts, magnetic shifts do not occur suddenly. The Earth is presently in the long process of a magnetic pole shift. According to Dr. Tony Phillips of NASA:

> Reversals take a few thousand years to complete and during that time—contrary to popular belief—the magnetic field does not vanish. . . . Magnetic lines of force near the Earth's surface become twisted and tangled, and magnetic poles pop up in unaccustomed places. A south magnetic pole might emerge over Africa, for instance, or a north pole over Tahiti.

Earth's magnetic field reverses its polarity periodically. The last time the magnetic field reversed was about 780,000 years ago. The time in between reversals is not consistent and can vary from a few hundred thousand years to millions of years. A magnetic reversal is likely to occur when the field is weak; however, over the last 12,000 years, the magnetic field has actually been lower than it is today.

There will be no magnetic reversal of the poles in 2012, although the internet is filled with uninformed opinions from amateurs who have no idea what they're talking about. Here is just one of hundreds of baseless assertions claiming that a pole shift will occur in 2012:

> In 2012, the next polar reversal will take place on Earth. This means that this North Pole will be changed into the South Pole. Scientifically, this can only be explained by the fact that the Earth will start rotating in the opposite direction, together with a huge disaster of unknown proportions. The Earth will be subjected to total destruction. It will be many times worse than my description. Terrible hunger, cold and pain, and more will rule your daily life without hope of a quick recovery because all resources will have been destroyed. This will be the reality of your daily life after the forthcoming polar reversal, and it is in this scenario you will have to try to survive.

Besides the author's inability to use proper grammar, he does not state any sources from which he has obtained this startling information. The only reference he cites is from "old Egypt" and "the secrets contained in the Labyrinth of Hawara". These claims have no merit whatsoever and can be filed under the category of "sheer fantasy." It is unfortunate that many people have been led to believe that such dire circumstances await them in 2012.

Coming back to reality, there is scientific research being conducted in an effort to understand the internal dynamics of our planet and the cause of a magnetic reversal. Dan Lothrop, a geophysicist from the University of Maryland, created his own spinning model of the Earth. He filled a 26-ton ball with a molten iron analogue and sodium to see whether the internal motion of this combined fluid could recreate a magnetic field (Kestenbaum, 2008).

In another unsubstantiated internet article, an author refers to the warnings of New Age authors to provide credibility for his claims:

> If we are looking at such an event which the likes of [new age author] affirms, then we are looking at three major events on the horizon.
>
>   1. earthquakes unlike anything we've seen
>
>   2. hurricanes from every direction
>
>   3. social unrest along with political and economic chaos

The author summarizes how easy it is to deceive the public:

> It's easy to speculate and it's even easier to come up with wild ideas about this 2012 shift; however, when renowned scientists begin to offer us the possibilities with "scientific data" to back them up—it might be time to step back and think.

The only thing to think about is what renowned scientists the author is referring to, and what scientific data is pointing to a pole shift in 2012. Obviously, the author has no credible evidence from the scientific community or, certainly, he would have stated his sources. Once again, another novice is attempting to frighten the public with an imaginary hypothesis.

Let's take a look at what scientists are *really* saying. According to a real scientist at NASA:

> This is one of the craziest lies that is being promulgated by the 2012 conspiracy theorists. It is totally absurd, and completely untrue, but still the story spreads and is frightening people. But

they frighten you by falsely claiming that a magnetic reversal is coming soon (like in 2012). There is no reason to expect a reversal of magnetic polarity anytime in the near future…a sudden shift in rotational poles with disastrous consequences is impossible… (http://astrobiology.nasa.gov/ask-an-astrobiologist/question /?id=4912 viewed March 23, 2010).

Geologist Brad Singer and paleomagnetist Kenneth Hoffmann analyzed samples of lava dating back 500,000-700,000 years from volcanoes in Tahiti and Germany and were able to deduce the direction of the magnetic field. The spin of the electrons in the mineral is apparently governed by the dominant magnetic field. During times of strong dipolar field, these electrons pointed toward the magnetic North Pole. During times of weak dipolar field, the electrons pointed to wherever the dominant field was, in this case the distributed magnetic field. This research team is of the opinion that when the weakened dipolar field drops below a certain threshold, the distributed field pulls the dipolar field off its axis, causing a geomagnetic shift (Sakai, 2009).

So, then, what does all this mean with regard to doomsday?

Some 2012 theories suggest that the Earth's geomagnetic reversal is connected to the natural 11-year solar cycle. However, there is no scientific evidence to support this claim either. So, this doomsday theory falters because a geomagnetic reversal does not occur with "clockwork regularity" and it has no connection with solar dynamics. Therefore, no one can predict the start date of such a phenomenon. Many experts say that, during the last one thousand years, about ten percent of the Earth's magnetic field has already shifted. During the next nine thousand years, the shift will be complete, and humanity will have plenty of time to adjust to this change in polarity.

Geomagnetic reversal is an engrossing area of geophysical research that will continue to occupy physicists and geologists

Pictorial representation of geomagnetic field reversal

for many years to come. However, there is absolutely no scientific evidence to support the claim that a geomagnetic reversal will be arriving just in time for December 21, 2012.

SOLAR FLARES SCORCH THE EARTH

Solar flares are tremendous explosions on the surface of the sun that occur near sunspots. The cause of solar flares is not completely understood. However, there appears to be a relationship between the sun's magnetic field and these sudden eruptions. One of the most plausible explanations for how solar flares are formed involves the interaction of the sun's magnetic fields moving in opposite directions against each other.

The sun has a natural cycle of solar flare activity that lasts for a period of 11 years. To understand the sun's 11-year cycle, it is necessary to consider the magnetic field lines of the sun. These lines loop around the sun, creating a kind of magnetic web, but are continuously changing in pattern and intensity during the solar cycle.

When some of these magnetic field lines become twisted (often in the vicinity of sunspots), energy builds up. When the magnetic energy of the sun reaches a certain point in the solar atmosphere, the pressure must be released. The release of this energy is a solar flare, which can produce radiation bursts from across the electromagnetic spectrum, from radio waves to x-rays and gamma-rays. The amount of this energy is equal to an explosion of tens of millions of atomic bombs exploding simultaneously.

There are three categories of solar flares. The largest flares are called X-class flares. They are rare, but can cause electrical blackouts around the Earth and inject radiation into the upper atmosphere. M-class flares (medium in size) are also uncommon and can cause brief blackouts; however, they do not affect 90 percent of the Earth's

Solar Flares

surface. Only minor radiation enters the atmosphere following this type of flare. C-class flares are the smallest and most common type and do not impact life on Earth. Therefore, the effects of solar flares are usually limited to interruptions in satellite communications, decreases in electrical output, and influences on weather patterns.

The effects of X-class X-ray flares can be felt on Earth within minutes. Geomagnetic storms reaching the Earth as a result of X-class flares have been associated with the March 6, 1989 disruption of Canada's power grid and the April 2, 2001 sighting of the aurora borealis as far south as Mexico (ESA and NASA 2006).

Trying to predict the occurrence of a massive solar flare is practically impossible. The sun does not give any advance warning about when such mega-flares are ready to explode. However, scientists point to areas of sunspots that may correlate with unusually large solar flare activity. Fortunately, the Earth will not be affected by even the largest of solar activity, because the magnetosphere and the ozone layer provide protection from these solar outbursts. Additionally, there is no need to worry about most solar flares since the majority of flares occur near the surface of the sun (corona).

Once in awhile a Coronal Mass Ejection (CME) can occur independently of a solar flare. This is a situation when the plasma of the sun is ejected from its surface. The CME can cause magnetic storms, and its gases can reach the Earth's magnetic field, although will not penetrate it. Because of this threat, we now have a number of space-based observatories that are tracking CMEs and give us advance warning if one is headed for the Earth.

Taking a look at a recent article on the internet, we find another misinformed prediction relating to destruction caused by solar flares:

> The Mayan calendar does certainly describe an end of times in 2012. If you do a couple of hours of research on the internet, you will find factual information that explains how we are certain to experience solar flare activity unlike any we have ever experienced before. This is what we face in 2012. . . . we could lose our power systems for a sustained length of time including all automobiles that have computer chips. A little worse: we could face radiation poisoning. We know for sure that solar flares in 2012 will exceed

any others that have come before. These flares could begin as soon as 2010 as we move closer to the center of the Milky Way.

Logic and common sense tell me the chances of losing power through this event are greater than 50%. We know that in 2012 we will have solar flares more extreme than have ever been recorded.

Fortunately, there are over 7,800 firms that supply electric power to US customers. Will solar flares, CMEs, and the like interrupt or bring down the North American power grid? No.

How much damage can we expect from solar storms in the current 11 year sun cycle? There are three stages leading to the formation of a solar flare. First, the magnetic energy is resulting in the emission of gamma rays. Second, there is an acceleration of protons and electrons that produce radio waves and gamma rays. Third, a degeneration of "soft X rays" are identified as the solar flare burns itself out.

The monthly average of visible sunspots indicates that the number of sunspots tends to fluctuate over an 11-year cycle (NASA, 2009). The sun is moving into another peak in its 11-year solar cycle, suggesting to 2012 doomsday enthusiasts the possibility of a huge solar flare licking-up the Earth and causing massive damage. In addition, the 11-year solar cycle seems to coincide with the cycles in the Mayan Calendar, possibly indicating the Mayas' close observation of the sun.

Although solar flares can cause damage to satellites and the occasional power outage, they are not powerful enough in themselves to destroy the Earth. Even the slim possibility of multiple near-simultaneous X-class flares and CMEs would not be powerful enough to penetrate the Earth's protective layers (the magnetosphere, ionosphere, and atmosphere) and do serious damage. Furthermore, the incident where a "killer" solar flare that was once observed originating from another star, could not arise from the sun because the sun is not the same type of star as the one involved in that massive flare (a red giant). Nor does our sun have a binary partner with which to interact in a gravitational interaction (http://earthobservatory.nasa.gov/Features/SORCE/sorce_03.php viewed March 23, 2010).

Therefore, those who predict a 2012 doomsday scenario cannot base their claim on a dramatic solar flare because our sun is a stable star with a fairly predictable 11-year cycle, and there is no evidence to indicate that solar flares have ever caused mass destruction on Earth.

PLANET X CRASHES INTO EARTH: TOTAL ANNIHILATION

The doomsayers have come up with another unverifiable theory for destroying our Earth in 2012. They have latched onto the idea that an unknown planet is orbiting our Sun every 3600 years and is on a collision course with Earth. This planet has been referred to as Planet X, and apparently, it gets its name from being a rather elusive planet.

According to some believers of Doomsday 2012, the first real pictures of Planet X were photographed shortly after January 26, 1983, when NASA launched the Infrared Astronomical Satellite (IRAS). The astronomers calculated that Planet X was over 50 million miles away from Earth at that time. The believers said that in 2004, Planet X would be only 7 million miles away. In other words, it is supposedly moving closer toward Earth. Furthermore, there is a prediction that Planet X will crash into the Earth at the end of 2012.

Here is the scenario presented in another way. It is now believed that the object in the IRAS photo of 1983 is the same as certain objects later discovered in Pluto's orbit in 1992 (which we will discuss later). While the object in the IRAS photo was thought to

Planet X crashes into Earth

be 50 billion miles from Earth, the objects observed in 1992 were thought to be 7 billion miles away. Thus, believers of Planet X theory claimed that this planet had traveled 43 billion miles in nine years and would complete the distance to Earth by 2003. When that event didn't happen, there arose a claim that a photograph of Planet X was taken in Japan on February 28, 2008. Now that *that* year has come and gone, they are focusing on 2012. But getting back to their original basis for these predictions, there is *no* explanation as to why it would take 11 years (for the original arrival date) or 20 years (for the revised date) for a planet to travel one-sixth as far as it had supposedly traveled in 9 years.

Whenever there is no scientific proof to support a hypothesis, there are always those who will turn to Biblical prophecy to justify their beliefs:

> From a far away land they came, from the end-point of Heaven
> do the Lord and his weapons of wrath come to destroy the whole
> Earth. Therefore, will I agitate the Heavens, and Earth shall be

shaken out of its place. When the Lord of Hosts shall be crossing, the day of his burning wrath will come (Isaiah 13:1).

And then there's the *Book of Revelation*, which has a plentiful supply of doomsday imagery:

> I watched as he opened the sixth seal. There was a great earthquake. The Sun turned black like sackcloth made of goat hair, the whole Moon turned blood red and the stars in the sky fell to Earth, as late figs drop from a fig tree when shaken by a strong wind.
>
> The sky receded like a scroll, rolling up, and every mountain and island was removed from its place. Then the kings of the Earth, the princes, the generals, the rich, the mighty, and every slave and every free man hid in caves and among the rocks of the mountains (Rev. 6:12-15).

However, the truth about Planet X is decidedly different from the story told by the doomsayers. After the discovery of Neptune in 1846, there was much speculation that another planet might exist beyond its orbit. The search for this "mystery planet" began with Percival Lowell's quest to find Planet X. He proposed the Planet X theory to explain the apparent discrepancies that were found in the orbits of Uranus and Neptune. He was speculating that the gravity of a large unseen planet could interact with the orbit of Uranus enough to account for these irregularities.

Subsequently, Clyde Tombaugh's discovery of Pluto in 1930 appeared to validate Lowell's hypothesis, and Pluto was officially considered the ninth planet until 2006. And yet, Pluto was found to be too small for its gravity to affect the much larger planets. Consequently, a brief search began for a tenth planet. However, the search was abandoned in the early 1990s when the Voyager 2 spacecraft found that irregularities observed in the orbit of Uranus were due to a slight over-estimation of Neptune's mass. This determination was made by Dr. Myles Standish of the Jet Propulsion Laboratory in Pasadena, California, in 1992. He used the data from Voyager 2's 1989 flyby of Neptune, which resulted in Neptune's total mass being revised downward to 0.5% (comparable to the mass of Mars). After this, the gravitational pull of Neptune on Uranus was in need of recalculation. When Neptune's newly determined mass was used in the Jet Propulsion Laboratory Developmental Ephemeris (JPL DE), the supposed discrepancies in the orbit of Uranus—and with them the need for a Planet X—vanished. Moreover, there have been no discrepancies in the trajectories of any space probes, such as Pioneer 10, Pioneer 11, Voyager 1, and Voyager 2, that can be attributed to the gravitational pull of a large, undiscovered object in the outer Solar System.

In 1992, the discovery of numerous icy objects within Pluto's orbit led to a debate over whether Pluto should maintain its status as a planet. Then the question arose as to whether Pluto and its neighbors should be given their own classification. In 2006, the International Astronomical Union reclassified Pluto and its largest neighbors as dwarf planets, leaving only eight planets in our Solar System. Nevertheless, some 2012 believers continue to emphasize the 1983 photograph taken by NASA's IRAS. A *Washington Post* article on this find stated:

> So mysterious is the object that astronomers do not know if it is a planet, a giant comet, a nearby "proto-star" that never got hot enough to become a star, a distant galaxy so young that it is still in the process of forming its first stars, or a galaxy so shrouded in dust that none of the light cast by its stars ever gets through (O'Toole, 1983).

As noted, the astronomers did not know what the object was, but according to a scientific article based on the early reports from which the *Washington Post* story was extracted:

A number of candidate identifications have been considered, including near-Solar System, galactic, and extragalactic objects. Further observations at infrared and other wavelengths may provide additional information in support of one of these conjectures, or perhaps these objects will require entirely different interpretations (Houck, *Astrophysical Journal Letters*, 1984).

This scientific publication did not support the idea of an object hurtling toward Earth or the existence of any unknown celestial bodies orbiting the outer reaches of our Solar System. Since these conclusions were not widely reported by the media, there are still many people who believe that Planet X is out there—somewhere.

The name *Nibiru* (alt. Niburu) is often associated with Planet X, and it is another "mystery planet" theory spoken of by Zecharia Sitchen. While Sitchen was researching the possibility of extraterrestrial intervention in early human development, he came across a theory of a 12th planet called Nibiru. With worldwide distribution of Sitchen's books on this subject, many of his followers have linked Nibiru to the idea of Planet X. According to the ancient (6000-3000 BCE) Sumerians, Nibiru was known as "Planet of the Crossing." However, there is no astronomical evidence for a link between Nibiru and Planet X, nor even the slightest bit of scientific evidence that Nibiru exists. The most interesting aspect of the Nibiru story is its possible association in Babylonian texts with the planet Jupiter. Nevertheless, there are plenty of "die-hard 2012 believers" who continue clinging to a connection between Nibiru and Planet X.

In order to present both sides of the story, here is a recent posting on the internet describing the destructive force of Planet X/ Nibiru.

What is Planet X? It could be a comet, a rogue planet, or a dying brown dwarf companion to the sun. In the years to come, it's elliptical orbit will bring it into the core of our system where it will enrage our sun. Once that happens, Earth's greatest pains will come at that moment. Fate puts us in the cross hairs of a perfect solar storm. The purpose of this new book is to help those who now agree that time is of the essence. It does this by offering a practical 2012 toolkit of how-to survival knowledge, for those who'll be left to fend for themselves. Regardless of whether you can afford to build a bunker or can barely afford a shovel, the information in this book is designed to be equally useful. This is because the key to surviving 2012 is more about what's in your head than what's in your wallet (*Planet X Forecast and 2012 Survival Guide*, 2007).

Today, most astronomers agree that Planet X, as Lowell defined it, does not exist. However, the concept of Planet X has been revived by a number of astronomers to explain other anomalies observed in the outer reaches of our Solar System. In popular culture and even among some astronomers, Planet X has become a substitute term for any undiscovered planet in our Solar System.

Chapter 10

CRYSTAL SKULLS AND OTHER PREDICTIONS

There is a theory that 13 crystal skulls will come together in 2012 and consequently, people will remember why their souls have come to Earth. As the story goes, thousands of years ago, 13 crystal skulls were hidden away by the Mayan Elders. They wanted future generations to discover them at "the fullness of time", at the end of the Mayan Long Count Calendar.

When it comes to objects such as pure quartz crystals, there are always plenty of myths and legends associated with them. Ancient civilizations were known to cut and polish beautiful rocks. They used quartz to produce crystal balls that they believed would show them the future. Furthermore, the early Mesoamericans thought the souls of the living and the dead were housed in crystals. This gave rise to the belief that some crystals were good while others were evil. A famous ancient legend tells of the original 13 crystal skulls, with jaws that were movable, that could sing and speak. Twelve of the skulls were symbolic of the sun, the moon, and the ten planets. The 13th is said to represent the rainbow feathered serpent god (Quetzalcoatl), who will return again to rule all the planets of our Universe. According to the myth, the crystal skulls are reservoirs of life's great secrets and offer information about the evolution of humanity. The myth predicts that a crisis will come, and the skulls will be rediscovered to reveal their hidden knowledge.

Mayan legend states that the 13 crystal skulls were originally kept in a pyramid. They were placed in a configuration of 12 forming a circle, with the 13th, and largest, skull being in the center. This Eye formation of the 13 crystal skulls was referred to as the *Ark*. The legend indicates that someday the skulls will reunite into the Ark formation, thereby causing a planetary elevation in consciousness. Interestingly, two other arks which are mentioned in the Bible— the ark of Noah and the Ark of the Covenant—are also related to the notion of new beginnings and heightened consciousness. One theory suggests that the formation of 12 crystal skulls positioned around a central one corresponds with the 12 tribes of Jacob/Israel; the 12 disciples/Jesus; and the 12 constellations/sun.

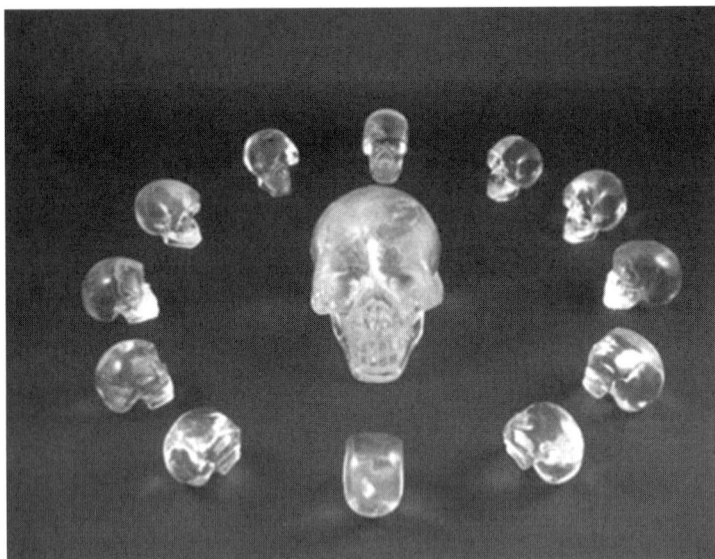

13 Crystal Skulls

The number 13 is the most important factor in this legend because it represents the governing body and a priestly king. It also symbolizes higher states of consciousness in other cultures, such as the Aztecs, the Pueblo, the Navajo, the Cherokee, and the Seneca.

The most controversial "discovery" of a crystal skull is the Mitchell-Hedges Skull, which was reportedly found in Central America in 1927. Mitchell-Hedges worked in an ancient Mayan settlement in a damp tropical jungle in Yucatan (currently Belize) in 1924. His team had decided to burn down 33 hectares of forest covering the ancient constructions of the settlement to make the archeological dig easier. When the smoke lifted, the explorers saw amazing ruins of a stone pyramid, city walls, and a huge amphitheatre capable of seating thousands of spectators. The ancient settlement was called *Lubaantun*, "The Place of the Fallen Stones."

Three years later, Mitchell-Hedges organized another trip, and this time he took his daughter Anna. On her 17th birthday, in April of 1927, Anna claimed to find a strange item under the debris of an ancient altar. It was a life-sized human skull made of crystal that sparkled in the light. This skull, which was about 5.25" high and weighed 11 pounds, was to become known as "the Skull of Doom". The skull lacked its lower jaw, which was found three months later about a dozen meters away from the original site. According to F.A. Mitchell- Hedges, the skull is 3,600 years old, and according to legend, it was used by the high priests of the Maya when performing esoteric rights.

Today, it is known that the discovery was a hoax. Those who were part of the Lubaantun excursion said that Mitchell-Hedges

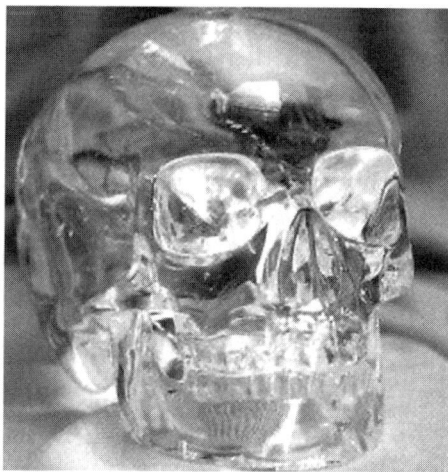

The Mitchell-Hedges Skull

and his daughter did not find a crystal skull on this trip. Rather, the crystal skull had been put up for auction, and Mitchell-Hedges had outbid the British Museum to acquire it. There is documentation at the British Museum which verifies this claim. However, the origin of the crystal skull is still attributed to Central America. Meanwhile, Anna has maintained for all these years that she did, indeed, discover the skull. Conversely, there is reason to doubt that she was ever even present on the Lubaantun expedition! Despite the controversy surrounding the skull and how it came into her possession, Anna has continued to claim that it came from outer space and was created in Atlantis.

Jane MacLaren Walsh, an anthropologist at the Smithsonian's Museum of Natural History who has devoted much of her career to the study of crystal skulls, contends:

> I believe all of the smaller crystal skulls that constitute the first generation of fakes were made in Mexico around the time they were sold, between 1856 and 1880. The Mitchell-Hedges skull, which appears after 1934, is a veritable copy of the British Museum skull, with stylistic and technical flourishes that only an accomplished faker would devise. So why have crystal skulls had such a long and successful run, and why do some museums continue to exhibit them, despite their lack of archeological context and obvious iconographic, stylistic, and technical problems? Though the British Museum exhibits its skulls as examples of fakes, others still offer them up as the genuine article. Mexico's National Museum, for example, identifies its skulls as the work of Aztec and Mixtec artisans. Perhaps it is because, like the Indiana Jones movies, these macabre objects are reliable crowd-pleasers (*Archeology*, vol 61:3, May/June 2008).

Today, many people see the crystal skulls metaphorically: as a hologram through which we can experience the virtual world.

However, for die-hard believers, there are still 12 pyramids or 12 significant points of power that are placed strategically around the globe. They are supposed to come to life when human consciousness awakens. Thus, when all 13 crystal skulls come together, humanity will remember the soul's purpose on Earth. At that time, a gradual transformation of evolutionary consciousness will begin. As already noted, the Mayan legend indicates that the 13 crystal skulls were left behind by Mayan elders in the hope that future generations would bring them together at the end of the Mayan Long Count Calendar.

THE BIBLE CODE

In the late 1990s, there was a claim of a hidden code within the Bible that is found through computer analysis of the Hebrew text. This theory was brought to the attention of the world in the best- selling book, *The Bible Code*, by Michael Drosnin. Believers in this "Bible Code" theory look at the Hebrew Bible as a continuation of letters without spaces and search for words that are formed by "equidistant letter sequences" (ELS). For example, the computer could randomly select every fourth letter and respond with an identification of a coded word that is intersecting with words relating to each other. Using this method, there are claims that the Bible is imbedded with predictions of the future. These include such events as the assassination of Israel's prime minister, Yitzhak Rabin, and an earthquake that will hit Los Angeles in 2010.

Here's how the Bible Code works. A starting point and a skip number are chosen, and letters are selected from the text at equal spacing (the skip number). For example, let's take a look at Genesis 31:28:

And hast not suffered me to kiss my sons and my *daughters? Thou hast now done foolishly* in so doing.

```
ERWASREALONTHEMORNINGOFSEPTEMBER
TEMBERIWASAWAKENEDBYTHEEVENTTHAT
NTTHATPROVEDTHREALSUDDENLYTHEREW
THEREWASNOROOMFORDOUBTITWASNTJUS
SNTJUSTISRAELITWASTHEUNITEDSTATE
DSTATESITWASNEWYORKITWASTHECITYW
ECITYWHEREILIVEDITWASJUSTDOWNTHE
OWNTHEBLOCKANDISAWITHAPPENWITHMY
WITHMYOWNEYESTHEATTACKONNEWYORKT
WYORKTHEATTACKONTHEWORLDTRADECEN
ADECENTERTHISUNBELIEVABLEHORRORW
ORRORWASNOTONLYENCODEDINTHEBIBLE
EBIBLEIHADACTUALLYSEENITINADVANC
ADVANCEIHADFOUNDITINRIGHTAFTERTH
FTERTHEFAILEDTERRORISTATTACKONTH
CKONTHESAMETWOTOWERSTWINTOWERSWA
WERSWASENCODEDINTHEBIBLEWITHTHEW
THTHEWARNINGTHESLAUGHTERANDTHATW
DTHATWASCROSSEDBYTERRORTERRORAPP
RORAPPEAREDASECONDTIMEANDITWILLF
TWILLFALLCOLLAPSEWASALSOENCODEDT
CODEDTWICEBUTIASSUMEDITWASABOUTT
ABOUTTHEPASTNOTTHEFUTUREITNEVERO
NEVEROCCURREDTOMETHATLIGHTNINGWO
NINGWOULDSTRIKETWICETHATTHEREWOU
EREWOULDBEANOTHERTERRORISTATTACK
ATTACKONTHESAMETWOMONOLITHSEIGHT
SEIGHTYEARSLATERTHATITWOULDSUCCE
```

Interpreting the The Bible Code

Accordingly, when the Hebrew letters are translated into English, a line of consecutive letters appears to complete the verse. Taking a segment of this verse, we start with the word "daughters." The computer identifies the first important letter, "R." Then, by skipping over three letters to the "O," and continuing to skip three letters thereafter, the "hidden message," *Roswell* appears:

D A U G H T E Rs th Ou h a St n o Wd on Ef o o Li s h Ly

In one reading of *The Bible Code*, a cluster of words and phrases were found supposedly concerning predictions for 2012:

comet large - stone-like / stony : object - sped / Tongue-like : Sun - whole earth / earth annihilated - smitten / stricken - smitten

Planetary / wanderer : fragmentary : sixty mile - blunderbuss /
scatter-gun / Crater : Canada : ultimate : terrifying : appalling
: lethal / Modifier - mantle - axis - tilting - tipping : Speeded /
Seismic - eradication - It will be crumbled / I will tear to pieces

Scholars of the Bible argue against *The Bible Code* because the
original version of the Bible does not exist. Even the oldest Bibles
have been translated from the Greek Septuagint and, therefore,
the computer results could not be accurate. A report from Jerusalem's Hebrew University states, "despite a considerable amount of
effort, we have been unable to detect any codes". In fact, the results
of this study found that the Hebrew translation of Tolstoy's *War
and Peace* yielded similar results as that of *The Bible Code*. However,
Drosnin has been quoted as saying, "I don't think the code makes
predictions. I think it reveals probabilities…. It might tell us all our
possible futures, which appears to include a warning of a possible
nuclear war."

There are many critics of *The Bible Code* who do not believe
it can predict the future. Others have accused Drosnin of laying
claim to scientific support that he does not have, and critics say he
mistranslates Hebrew words to strengthen his case. Additionally,
a public statement has been issued by more than fifty professional
mathematicians and statisticians who found that there is no evidence to support the methodologies of *The Bible Code*.

According to an article by researcher Brendan McKay, professor at the Department of Computer Science at Australian National
University, "Michael Drosnin's new book, *Bible Code II-The Countdown*, exceeds the first one in stupidity. A large part of the book is
concerned with a pathetic, futile search for some 'obelisks' contained
in a 'steel ark' supposedly left on Earth by some superior intelligence
in the distant past. It is interesting that Drosnin has decided to
rewrite the history of the codes in this book, even contradicting his
first book."

As with other disaster theories, there is speculation on the internet about the validity of *The Bible Code* and its predictions. Drosnin has been somewhat successful in convincing many of his readers that he has uncovered an authentic code-breaking technique. Here is an example of a *Bible Code* believer who is spreading the word about this highly questionable theory:

> The code has been verified by both mathematicians and code-breakers to be quite real. Furthermore, the last encoded date (thus far established) is the seventh month of 2126, when comet Swift-Tuttle, is expected to return to the vicinity of the Earth. In the interim, however, is the prediction of another comet due in 2012, which is expected to crumble into pieces or "annihilate" the Earth.

Thanks for the warning!

OTHER PREDICTIONS BY MODERN WRITERS

It seems as though the 2012 doomsayers are everywhere. The following (anonymously presented) excerpts are from two typical postings found on the internet by individuals who are "buying into" the 2012 end of time propaganda. There are hundreds of such individuals creating blogs on the internet, who are absolutely sure the world is ending in 2012 because of what they have been led to believe by the media, various authors, "authorities" on the lecture circuit, and a blockbuster Hollywood film. These postings are complete with dire predictions of earthquakes, tsunamis, hurricanes, and volcanoes. The first makes a number of references to the many doomsday hypotheses discussed earlier:

> Ancient Mayan records clearly provide warning to future civilizations by stating the end of the long count Galactic Cycle in the

early 21st century will mark the end of an age in which global catastrophes will begin. They refer to the next cycle as the fifth cycle and the period of purification.

As we approach the gravitational plane, we will continue to experience severe weather and ecological affects [sic] such as earthquakes, tsunamis, hurricanes, and volcanic activity with increased frequency and intensity. As we penetrate the densest portion of the Galactic Plane and experience the full gravitational affects [sic], we may witness unprecedented solar flares, unexpected meteor showers, and one or more geographical pole shifts. Subsequently, unexpected celestial objects may pass through the Solar System as they, too, are influenced by the gravitational plane. This may account for the ancient records' describing several past worldwide catastrophes accompanied by passing bodies or comets, or what some researchers today refer to as Planet X.

So, if these ancient civilizations knew what was coming over the horizon due to cyclic patterns and scientific calculations we have lost through one of history's gaps, than [sic] what exactly was it that they knew? Even if pole shifts take place in a cyclic pattern, they don't occur on their own.

Since a geographical pole shift would most likely result in a permanent change in the axis of the Earth, the affects [sic] would also have immediate implications on global climate, causing new weather patterns and regional temperature changes. Places that were once desert might now be plush [sic]. Or, areas that were once abundant with vegetation and life may become a frozen wasteland: areas like Antarctic.

The calendar advances, galactic forces move into alignment, the Mayan prophecy approaches. In the aftermath of downfall, a new order emerges. In fact, the Mayan calendar suggests that after the year 2012 a new Dark Age will emerge.

Elsewhere on the internet, an author focuses exclusively on Planet X as a culprit:

> In 1983, NASA scientists found the existence of another planet in our Solar System. They did not know what it was at the time, so they called it "Planet X."
>
> Planet X is supposedly the ancient planet Nibiru. This outer planet rotates through our Solar System every 3,600 years. When Nibiru comes close enough to us, the Earth will stop spinning for at least one week. This will cause: tsunamis, floods and killer waves all over the coasts of the world, hurricanes, earthquakes, and volcanoes. There is no way we can stop this from happening.
>
> When Planet X hits the Earth, two-thirds of the world's population will perish. Eventually, many of the survivors will die from the effects of disasters, starvation, and thirst. We have to face reality and try to save ourselves if our species is to survive. Scientists are investigating ways to save the Earth, but until something is done, we are on our own. World army bases are planning to build camps to save people, but have not started construction yet.
>
> There is a small line between life and death; we either live or die. Do you want to survive 2012 by preparing properly, or do you want to be caught off-guard and live through another stone age?

These articles do not present a very optimistic picture for 2012. Therefore, we must ask for scientific data to support the hundreds of doomsday scenarios on the internet. Fortunately, you will not find any credible evidence to back-up these claims.

Chapter 11

ANCIENT ASTRONAUTS

The belief that extraterrestrials visited Earth and influenced the development of human culture, religion, and history, is known as *ancient astronaut theory*. More specifically, this theory states that many of the gods depicted in various cultures were actually ancient astronauts. Some ancient astronaut proponents say that these aliens could have created the first human beings. While these theories are highly speculative, they have been popularized by authors such as Erich von Daniken and Zecharia Sitchin. These writers, who argue in favor of ancient astronaut theory, point to technological innovations displayed in archeological artifacts. They insist that ancient cultures could not have left behind such magnificent monuments, pyramids, and temples. The most compelling evidence in support of this theory is creation mythology, which describe gods descending from the sky. These stories include references to "divine beings" with supernatural abilities, who interact with mortals.

Erich Von Daniken is an author of several books on this subject, and claims that many of the myths of ancient civilizations were introduced by higher intelligences. For example, in Sanskrit epics from India, flying machines—*Vimanas*—are depicted. These references to supernatural abilities (such as the Mayan ruler Pacal depicted in a space ship) are interpreted by Von Daniken as an example of extraterrestrial technology.

Likewise, in the Hebrew Bible, God is sometimes portrayed as a burning bush, a moving cloud, a whirlwind of fire, and a thunderous voice. In the *Book of Ezekiel*, God is described as a "figure on a throne, like that of a man, but the upper portion is like glowing metal with fire all around it. The lower portion is like fire, and there was a multi-colored glow all around Him, like a rainbow, the sign of hope" (Ezekiel 1:26-28). Ezekiel also speaks of a dark, flashing cloud of judgment that includes symbols of peace and hope.

These Biblical references can be interpreted as an E.T. playing the part of God. However, Ezekiel is speaking of a "vision" and, his description of events is subjective and possibly surreal. Ezekiel gives us tantalizing clues that invite us to investigate this matter further, however no definitive conclusion can be reached. Whether a "divine being" or an E.T. is sitting atop of the Merkabah, no one will ever know.

Other examples of possible alien visitations include the Greek myth of Prometheus who brought fire to mortals. Also included are the Incas' Viracocha who brought great mystical powers, and Kukulcan who gave the Mayas the secrets of agriculture and medicine.

Most importantly, the lid on Pacal's sarcophagus in Palenque appears to represent an astronaut inside his space capsule. In 1952, this interpretation was offered by Soviet scientist Alexander Kazantev, who believed the carving on the lid depicted a man who looked like an astronaut heading off into space. However, Mayan legend states that the carving on the sarcophagus illustrates King Pacal falling into the jaws of the Earth monster each night and arising again the next morning with the power of the Sun.

This hypothesis was widely circulated in the 1970s in a television documentary by *Twilight Zone* creator, Rod Serling. In this documentary, Serling points out that many ancient cultures have left behind super-human achievements, such as statues of giant faces on Easter Island and cave carvings that portray alien-like figures.

Advocates for ancient astronaut theory believe that the phenomenal architectural achievements of ancient civilizations went beyond the capabilities of human beings at that time. Also, among the unexplained artifacts, there are engravings that depict the Earth orbiting around the sun, and the understanding that the moon was

Sarcophagus Lid of Pacal at Palenque

reflecting the light of the sun. Furthermore, believers in ancient astronaut theory claim that the theory of evolution applies to other planets in the universe, and therefore, some species will be more advanced than our own.

As can be expected, there are many critics of ancient astronaut theory. Most criticism is leveled at Erich von Daniken and Sitchin by the scientific and academic communities. For example, von Daniken was denounced for claiming his photographs were of ancient pottery engraved with images of flying saucers. Investigators from Nova, a well-respected public television series, were able to locate the artist who created "ancient pottery." When von Daniken was confronted with evidence of this deception, he said his actions were justified because people would only believe in ancient astronauts if there was "proof"! Von Daniken was also the first writer to bring the world's attention to the Sarcophagus Lid of Palenque. He claimed that this Mayan engraving was a critical piece of evidence to corroborate his ancient astronaut theory. However, according to Maya glyph expert Ian Graham, "I certainly don't see any need to regard him as a space man. I don't see any oxygen tubes. I see a very characteristically drawn Maya face."

Many questions still remain about the validity of ancient astronaut theory. Specifically, there are many authentic remnants that illustrate flying machines and alien-like creatures. In addition, credible explanations are needed to understand how the pyramids were built, and why there were huge leaps in technological advancements over short periods of time. Although the evidence for ancient astronaut theory is not overwhelming, it is a possible answer for solving some of the world's ancient mysteries.

NAZCA LINES OF PERU

Aside from prophecies, crystal skulls, alien visitations, and cosmic disasters, there is cryptic evidence around the world that is linked to the story of 2012. Some of the most intriguing remnants from the past are the Peruvian Nazca lines.

The Nazca lines are at least 1,500 years old. They contain mysterious symbols and many people believe they relate to the Mayan prophecies for 2012. The Nazca lines and figures cover a total area of 520 square kilometers. They are located 400 kilometers south of Lima on a desolate plain between the Peruvian Coast and the Andes Mountains.

The Nazca Lines of Peru.
(Picture courtesy: http://www.zmescience.com)

Several mysteriously stylized figures are etched into the rocky terrain throughout the area. These figures are gigantic. The largest measures 285 meters in length, and there are 70 figures that resemble animals, geometric shapes, and floral patterns.

Among the largest animal figures are the:

+ spider (46m)

+ monkey (55m)

+ guanay bird (280m)

+ lizard (180m)

+ hummingbird (50m)

+ whale (65m)

+ pelican (285m)

Many researchers studying the Nazca lines point out that most of the creatures represent figures that are not native to the area. For example, the 45-meter long spider is identified as a member of the rare genus Ricinulei, which is found only in the most inaccessible parts of the Amazon Jungle. In reality, these spiders are only 5-10 millimeters in length, with one leg noticeably longer than the others—like a protruding tube. The Nazca spider clearly shows this extended leg.

Overlaying the figures are 800 straight lines that stretch over the landscape of the entire area. While some of these lines continue for 8 kilometers, one of them is an incredible 65 kilometers long. It is apparent that the drawings of the figures were created first, followed by the long, straight lines that cut right through them.

The Nazca lines were first noticed by pilots in the 1920s. In 1941, Dr. Paul Kosok of Long Island University was sent to survey them. At the site, Dr. Kosok found a rock carving of a bird which was the first discovery of an animal figure at Nazca. He realized that most of the lines fanned out from "radiating centers" and concluded that these lines had astronomical implications. Dr. Kosok understood it would take several years to survey the Nazca lines. Since he was working on several other projects and didn't have the time to study the figures properly, he handed over the project to his assistant, Maria Reiche, who had moved to Peru in 1932. Initially, she made brief visits to the lines from her home in Lima, but eventually became increasingly dedicated to solving the enigma of the Nazca lines. She wanted to devote full time to unravel the meaning of the figures, so she moved to a nearby ranch. After spending a decade examining these mysterious shapes, she decided to live on-site and dedicate the remaining 50 years of her life to deciphering the Nazca lines.

Reiche was the first person to discover the other animal figures, which were not visible until she cleared away the dust that had accumulated over many centuries. Additionally, she agreed with Dr. Kosok that the meaning of the figures was derived from astronomy.

Aside from the straight lines at the Nazca site, Reiche also found triangles, "needle and thread" patterns, trapezoids, a maze, and spirals. Incredibly, there are more than one hundred spirals at the site. Near the center of one of them, Reiche found a stone engraved with a serpent design and a severed head. Her conclusion was that every spiral at Nazca represents a serpent.

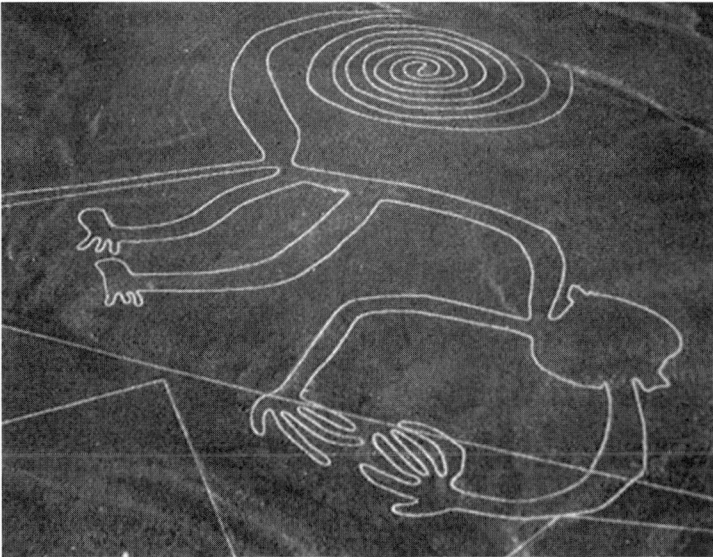

Close-up aerial view of Nazca lines – Peru

Reiche's contribution was significant because she took an active role in protecting the lines. She prohibited vehicles from driving all over the area, which could have ruined the site. Today, the Nazca lines are a "world cultural heritage site" as pronounced by UNESCO.

Although the Nazca lines present an interesting research subject, there is no direct connection between the Nazca lines and 2012, and there is no evidence that the Nazcas and the Mayas shared any secret knowledge. However, there is one theory linking together the end of the Mayan Calendar with the Nazca lines: a connection to the stars. According to William H. Isbell, writing for *Scientific American:*

> As Reiche has pointed out for many years, certain Nazca lines mark the position of the sun at the summer and winter solstices, and certain other lines also appear to have calendrical significance. A computerized analysis of line orientation conducted by Hawkins failed to demonstrate that a majority of the lines have astronomical significance, and showed that twice as many of them were oriented with respect to annual solar and lunar extremes than would be expected on the basis of chance.

Scholars are still divided as to whether the Nazcas produced these lines. The remarkable size of these shapes suggests they were meant to be viewed from high above, however, the figures can also be recognized from the ground. Although it is possible that the Nazca lines were markers for alien intelligences, it is much more likely that the Nazca artisans were carving figures to be seen by their gods. It is difficult to find any other logical explanation as to why the Nazcas would have painstakingly engraved these lines into the rocky ground.

CROP CIRCLES AND 2012

The term crop circle was included in the Oxford Dictionary in 1990. Crop circles are distinct patterns or designs created by the flattening of crops in large fields that are visible from higher ground. Initially, two men from South Hampton, England, were credited with creating crop circles, but this story was debunked when ornate crop circles began appearing throughout the world. The designs that were found in 1981 were only simple circles.

In 1999, researcher Colin Andrews spent two years investigating this phenomenon. He found that 80 percent of the circles were probably man-made, but 20 percent remained a mystery. Over the last few years, crop circles with Mayan symbols have appeared over the British countryside. Many believe these circles are sending a message from an unknown source, pointing to a time of transition in 2012.

The Mayan Wheel, Silbury Hill, Wiltshire, August, 2004

As seen in the crop circle above, the ancient Mayas encoded their calendrical information into the Pyramid of Kukulcan at Chichen Itza. Another crop circle relating to Mayan astronomy is a star shaped hieroglyph at Etchilhampton Hill which relates to the planet Venus. This Mayan glyph is known as Lamat, or Venus as the evening star. In August, 2005, it was speculated that the Mayan calendrical numbers and the date of the solar zenith conjunction of Venus and the Pleiades was imbedded within a circle that was found in Waylands Smithy, Oxfordshire. It has been reported that this circle also includes information about the Venus transit of June 5-6, 2012. These claims are highly controversial, and crop circle researchers are still debating the true meaning of these symbols.

Other circles relating to Venus include a thirteen fold star appearing at Huish, Wiltshire in 2003, and a circle formation appearing at Longwood Warren, Wiltshire in 1995, showing the asteroid belt, the sun, and the orbits of Mars and Venus. This configuration later took place on 1/16/98, during an inferior conjunction of Venus. Also, a formation was found at Silbury Hill, Wiltshire, in 2002. A pentagram is shown as the orbit formed by Venus over five of its 584 day cycle.

These crop circles relating to the movements of Venus are of great importance due to the sacred nature of this planet among the Mayans. There are also other circles found in the fields of England that show detailed renderings of the Tzolk'in or 260 day Mayan calendar. Another circle was found in 1996 that illustrates the divine symbol of the Mayan creator god, Hanab Ku. This configuration is known as the Galactic Butterfly circle that the Mayans believed represented the source of all life in the Universe. The Hanab Ku crop circle is one of the most significant formations relating to 2012. According to Mayan mythology, Hanab Ku is not only the creator god, but also the Mother Womb which continually gives birth to new star systems and galaxies. The Mayas believed that Hanab Ku gave birth to the sun and the Earth and all the planets in our Solar System. They believed that this "eternal parent" releases bursts of consciousness at the end of each age.

Additionally, the Mayas believed that Hanab Ku controlled time, and their calendar systems were simply measuring natural time according to its original design. Therefore, when the Mayan calendar ends on December 21, 2012, the natural sequence of moments will continue, which forms the basis of time as we enter into a new calendrical cycle. The Mayan astronomers believed that humanity would have many new beginnings. The appearance of the Hanab Ku Galactic Butterfly crop circle reaffirms the significance of Mayan cosmology and its target date of 2012.

Mayan Calendar Crop Circle
Wayland's Smithy, Oxfordshire, August, 2005

Mayan 2012 Crop Circle
Woolstone Hill, Oxfordshire, August, 2005

Mayan Headdress Crop Circle
Silbury Hill, Wiltshire, July, 2009

Chapter 12

A New Age for 2012

The phrase "New Age" has been bantered about over the last 40 years to the point where it has lost its original meaning as a time of higher consciousness. In many instances, this once trendy term has become associated with questionable practitioners who have knowingly made false promises while asking for a handsome fee. Even the popular magazine, *The New Age Journal* decided to change its name to *Body & Soul* in 2002, to distance itself from the tarnished reputation of "new age" merchandise and marketers. Conversely, "new age" as described by the Mayas, connotes the upcoming time cycle of era-2012 which has no affiliation with the New Age Movement of the 1970s.

As spoken of by the Mayan Elders, the term "new age" refers to the beginning of a "new" 5,125 year "age" which was meticulously calculated to measure the progression of natural or cosmic time. The Mayas understood the difference between living in natural time versus living within a contrived system of months that honored the Greek and Roman gods (the Hellenic, Julian and Gregorian calendars). However, in the Mayan calendrical system, they divided their mega-cycle of 25,625 years into many sub-divisions. One of these mini-cycles covers a period of 144,000 days (also a significant number in *The Book of Revelation*) and is known as a baktun. The world entered the current baktun cycle immediately after Pope Gregory introduced the 12 month calendar system in 1582. According to the Mayan sage Valum Votan, the implementation of the Gregorian calendar (and 12 hour/60 minute clock) has affected the synchronistic rhythms of nature, and consequently, has caused an error in time. He also claims that discordant vibrations between natural and artificial time-keeping systems have separated humanity from the harmonious frequencies of the physical world. In fact, present day Mayan time-keepers argue that the Gregorian calendar and the clock are not based on logic, science, or nature, and they create the impression that time is linear, containable, and separate from the organic, flowing process of life.

The invention of the clock gave birth to the notion that time lies outside our physical bodies. The Mayas believe that our constant awareness of the clock defies the laws of nature and upsets world balance and is delaying the evolutionary development of our senses.

With this type of thinking, the organic, flowing process of life cannot be synchronized with nature. The Mayas believe that our constant adherence to the clock must be overcome before spiritual advancement can take place.

In 1637, Rene Descartes, the philosopher who said, "I think, therefore I am," placed a ceiling on the perception of time with his three dimensional concept of time and space. The coordinates of X, Y, and Z rendered a fourth dimension obsolete and created conflict with the Mayan view of time and space. At that moment, time was reduced from its qualitative essence to that of a quantity. In other words, anyone seeing through the lens of a linear grid was adopting a limited perception of time. The paradigms of ancient Mayan society are still studied and interpreted with these limitations in place. Therefore, as per the rules of modern day science, if something cannot be seen, touched, or proven with measurements, it does not exist.

With the coming of 2012, we are invited to remember the inner wisdom of natural time and our intuitive feelings toward space, motion, and duration. Accordingly, there are essential cycles of time that are found within our bodies and within nature's daily rhythms. Time is the ever-changing and unfolding "now" as it continually synchronizes itself with the whole, living Universe.

LIVING IN NATURAL TIME

Pacal Votan was one of the strongest influences on the Mayas. He was another god-man who arrived from across the Atlantic Ocean on a boat with his followers. He wore a long robe, had a beard, and is believed to have authored the *Popol Vuh*.

Valum Votan is also known as the "Closer of The Cycle". Among the Mayas, he is considered the final messenger of Pacal Votan's prophecy. He thought the fulfillment of human destiny would occur when humanity returned to natural time and relied on the synchronization of the 13 moon, 28 day calendar. This ancient, harmonic, and accurate system of time-keeping is supposed to cause a future transition into higher consciousness. As we pass through the final years of the present age, it is important for our thought patterns to be in harmony with nature. It is said that the 13 moon calendar of the Mayas will help us re-harmonize ourselves with the natural patterns of Earth and the stars.

It is highly unlikely that our Gregorian calendar will change anytime soon. However, as bizarre as it may sound, we can learn to live (within the schedule of our lives) according to a new calendar that flows with the ebb and tide of the Universe. As Valum Votan states, "It is the untried solution; the harmonic solution." Although the world around us will continue to observe the standard 12 month calendar, there is nothing to prevent us from being acutely aware of the natural harmonics associated with the accuracy of the 13 moon calendar.

Overlaying the perfect framework of the 13 moon calendar is another layer of natural time, known as "the sacred count of days". It is a cycle of 260 days that flows through the year. This sacred cycle, as developed by the ancient Mayas, is composed of 260 distinct energies that are called the Galactic Spin Cycle. It is the modern version of the ancient Mayan Tzolk'in calendar (Short Count), and it puts us directly in touch with the creational energies that comprise our inner and outer worlds.

There is great benefit derived from using the Tzolk'in calendar as a harmonic module. It serves as a map of the 260 energetic portals of self-inquiry, and we'll be able to see more deeply within ourselves. We'll also come to know the purpose of our lives and what each moment holds in store for us. Additionally, we'll listen to the inner guidance that is calling out to us, and will perceive important clues that are necessary for making future decisions.

As we surrender to the natural flow of life's timing, we are illuminated by the universal frequency of synchronization. By following the 13 moon calendar, we'll always be in the right place at the right time. Eventually, we'll come together with others to discuss the importance of living in a synchronized and peaceful world. According to Valum Votan, "We are the Peacemakers we have been waiting for!"

Pacal Votan left a universal message for future generations. He said, "If humanity wishes to save itself from world destruction, it must return to living in natural time." Although he was not speaking about 2012, he envisioned a future society that would suffer as a result of collective divergence from natural law. Votan predicted not only the evolution of an accelerated technological society, but also the resulting planetary damage that would follow in the aftermath. Furthermore, he spoke of an imbalance in nature that would threaten life on Earth unless the proper steps were taken to restore the health of the planet. Pacal Votan's prophetic call should awaken humanity to its collective responsibility to replenish and nourish our Earth.

THE POPOL VUH AND 2012

There are no specific citations in the *Popol Vuh* that refer to a cataclysmic event occurring in 2012. However, by reading the text, it becomes clear that the Mayas had a deep understanding of nature and how it works in accordance with time-cycles. They understood that floods, hurricanes, earthquakes, tornados, and natural eruptions will occur periodically, however, *they did not leave any written records indicating that a future disaster is coming in 2012.*

Since the *Popol Vuh* and the *Chilam Ba'lam* do not contain any dire predictions for 2012, it is important to look for warnings about the 'end of times' in *The Dresden Codex*. In 1739 CE, this text was found in Dresden, Germany and was aptly named *The Dresden Codex*. It includes the Mayan Short Count Calendar (Tzolk'in) of 260 days, along with hieroglyphs of certain gods who are associated with the dates of religious rituals. Additionally, detailed astronomical observations are recorded in this codex including Venus passages, dates of eclipses, planetary movements, and the expected days of equinoxes and solstices.

On the last page of the Dresden Codex, there is a colorful depiction of the goddess, Chac Chel (Ix Chel), who is pouring a bucket of water over a Lord of the Underworld. This controversial illustration has been interpreted by contemporary authors as indisputable proof that a worldwide flood is coming in 2012. A recent television documentary on *The Dresden Codex* attempted to explain the meaning of the goddess and the dragon who are pouring water over the Earth:

> The last page of The Dresden Codex shows the destruction of the world via water. Waves gush from the mouth of a celestial dragon. More flood waters pour from sun and moon symbols on the underside of the monster's body. An aged goddess also pours flood water onto the Earth. At the bottom of the picture crouches a ruler of the Under World. Above the picture, about half of the 15 glyphs have been destroyed, but a few of the remaining ones consistently refer to "Black Earth" or "Black on High" (*Decoding the Past*, History Channel, 2009).

After the airing of this program, a group of Mayan Elders spoke out against the inflammatory nature of the documentary. The Elders denounced any disaster theory that is linked to the end of the current cycle, and accused certain authors of distorting history. The Elders say that the year 2012 is irrelevant, and claim that most information on this subject is unreliable and contradictory. As for the illustration on the last page of the *Dresden Codex*, there is no specific date mentioned, and no indication that a flood will occur in 2012. Additionally, just because a goddess is pouring a jar of water over a mythical figure, it does not necessarily connote the coming of a worldwide flood. Accordingly, other interpretations emphasize the importance of the rainy season, and the role of the goddess in Mayan cosmology. Significantly, the *Dresden Codex* contains several references to the timing of agriculture and the expected times for heavy rains dates during the growing season.

Finally, a third interpretation refers to the similarity between the Mayan goddess pouring a jar of water, and the Egyptian man pouring a pitcher of water—known as Aquarius.

Since there are many parallels between the Mayas and the Egyptians (pyramids, hieroglyphics, astronomy, etc.), this correspondence is worthy of serious consideration. If both of these water-bearer signs have similar meanings, it can be surmised that the Mayan goddess, Chac Chel, is symbolizing a star constellation like her counterpart, Aquarius. Taking this one step further, we find that Aquarius is not a symbol for a worldwide flood—so correspondingly—the Mayan goddess is not a symbol for a 2012 flood. Unfortunately however, she has become the poster-child for certain writers who need proof to support their notion that a flood is coming in 2012.

It is evident that these authors are desperate to latch onto anything that will signal the "end of times." They have been trying to find "the smoking gun" for 2012 in Tabasco, Mexico, at an archeological

Aquarius

site known as Tortuguero. At this location, there are old monuments with great historic value, however, most of the inscriptions
(c. 650 CE) refer to battles won and names of rulers. Taking a look at
Monument 6, an interesting inscription translates as, "at the end of
the 13th baktun" (2012); and the next word is, "utom" or "it will happen"; followed by an indecipherable inscription; and the last word is
"yem" or "will descend." This partial sentence seems to predict the
return of the Mayan god, Bolon Yukte in era-2012. Interestingly,
the return of this mythological god is written in a hopeful manner,
and there is no indication that it is an end of the world prophecy
for 2012.

Especially annoying are modern authors who claim that natural disasters will always occur at the end of each Mayan Age. They
rationalize their doomsday scenarios by asserting that December
21, 2012 marks the end of an age, and therefore, it is assumed that
a disaster must follow. Now, if that's the best line of reasoning these

writers can offer, then it's safe to say that the new Age of the Fifth Sun will be ushered in with a whisper.

Again, that is another 2012 doomsday scenario that is not supported by scholarship or the Mayan texts. Many contemporary writers are so busy looking for predictions of world disasters that they have forgotten about the true meaning of 2012. We have already established that the cycles of the Mayan calendar do not speak of destruction, but rather the beginning of a new age that brings about creation, rebirth, and global awakening. By following this line of thinking and examining the essential concepts of spiritual evolution, the ultimate meaning of 2012 will be found.

THE NEXT GREAT CYCLE

According to the end of the Mayan calendar, the completion of the precession of the equinoxes will begin a new 26,000 year cycle of stellar progression. Native civilizations across the globe have equated their next great cycle of time with the concept of a Golden Age. These cultures and religions include the Sumerians, Egyptians, Kabbalists, Essenes, Chinese, Tibetans, Hindus, Elders of Peru, Navajo, Hopi, Cherokee, Apache, Iroquois, Dogon Tribe, and Aborigines.

As fervent stargazers, the ancient Mayas followed their 25,625 year Long Count Cycle, which is similar to the 25,920 year Egyptian Zodiac Cycle. These astrological "clocks" were designed to tell stories about different aspects of ancient life, and each star constellation marked the passing of one cosmic month within the grand cosmic year. Accordingly, many other traditions refer to this same 26,000 year cycle in their mystical time-keeping systems.

Fortunately, the Mayas left behind superhuman-sized stone monuments and pyramids that explain the precise computations relating to their calendar. They inscribed important stelae dates to ensure that future generations would know when the end of the cosmic year had arrived. It is interesting to note that this same 26,000 year cycle corresponds to the sun's orbit around Alcyone, which is the central star of the Pleiades constellation. As previously discussed, a Mayan legend states that this great civilization believed they came from the Pleiades. It is still not clear why the Mayas felt such a strong affinity with this constellation. However, the implications are fascinating and this story warrants further investigation.

As we approach the next great cycle, the Fifth Mayan World will become a synthesis of the previous four. This next period, called *Caban* by the Mayas is also referred to as *olien* in Aztec. Interesting, in the Mayan language, the word "ol", of *ollin*, means consciousness. Therefore, the upcoming cycle of the Fifth Sun connotes a shift into higher evolutionary consciousness. The date that Earth entered into the Fourth World is written as 0.0.0.0.0. in Mayan Long Count notation. All numbered dates from this point forward are moving toward the end of the 5,125 year age. Therefore, in future years beyond 2012, a new Long Count Cycle will begin, and numerically

Pleiades, star cluster in Taurus

all the numbers go back to zero, beginning a new world age, or "a new creation." According to Mayan sage Don Ramon Carbala:

> This is the fourth time that cycle convergence has come. This is the story of Mother Earth and us as her children. In reality, this is the planet's purpose. We are now faced with a real opportunity to reach the next level, which is not Fire, Earth, Air, or Water, not a time of polar opposites (hot/cold, light/dark, feminine/masculine, day/night), but a time when things will work together in harmony. Once this cycle is established, there will be unity between men and women, and between human beings and Mother Earth (Barrios, *The Book of Destiny*,2009).

We can only hope that most people are looking forward to the day when humanity will live together in unitary consciousness. The Long Count Calendar predicts that the time for world change will be coming soon, and humanity will have the opportunity to transcend its current state of reality. The "choice point" will come in 2012, and the collective consciousness of the planet will manifest itself accordingly.

> We can indeed achieve this balance and bring humanity to a spiritual level, a new order of understanding, and transcend from this space-time to other dimensions, other levels we can't even begin to imagine; we can start down a new path within existence, structuring and creating the Universe (2009).

WHAT'S NEXT? A MESSAGE FROM THE MAYAN ELDERS

Even though we might like to think so, December 21, 2012, will probably not be the day when a light bulb is suddenly switched on and everyone's life becomes perfect in an instant. In fact, the Mayas believe that we are in the process of a gradual transition from one world into the next. Just look around you and you'll see that major changes in daily life are underway, and these positive influences will continue accelerating as we head into the final countdown to 2012.

The Mayan Elders believe that a spiritual awakening is coming in era-2012. They point to the end of the Long Count Calendar as a time of transition and acceptance among all nations. They say that people will embrace ancient spiritual wisdom and realize that all is one. Consequently, the walls of dogmatic religions will continue to crumble, and most people will consider themselves to be "spiritual" but not "religious." It is likely the future generations will look back at the religious stories of our time and interpret them symbolically (as parables).

As discussed, the Mayas were astute time-keepers and understood the nature of pivotal turning points within the time frame of a grand cycle. Their extraordinary knowledge of planetary orbits, seasons, and Earth changes was based on hundreds of years of observation and experience. They used 17 different calendars and were able to measure cycles of time that continued for millions of years into the future. The Elders maintain that Mayan predictions for the next cycle are filled with hope, optimism, and spiritual renewal. According to Carlos Barrios:

> Anthropologists visit the temple sites and read the inscriptions. Then, they make up stories about the Maya because they do not read the signs correctly. It's just their imagination. Other people write about prophecy in the name of the Maya. They say that the world will end on December 21, 2012. The Mayan Elders are angry with us because the world will not end—it will be transformed (Hall, 2009).

WHAT WILL HAPPEN TO YOU IN 2012?

According to the Mayan Elders, you will experience a new way of thinking as 2012 approaches. You will experience an increased sense of self-perception that will transcend your former limitations. A change will occur in receptivity that will open your mind to future possibilities. The need to control every minute of your life will come to an end, and you'll begin to trust the rhythm of nature. You will finally allow life to unfold as it should and let life happen. Once you are living in harmony with natural time, you will find that the momentum to life moves by itself. You will be swept up in the movement of total Being, and you will let go of ideas that no longer work. You'll understand there is no specific destination that awaits you other than where you are. Your former knowledge of yourself will be released and replaced with no knowledge at all.

Once you have emptied yourself of false ideas imposed upon you by family, friends, and society, you will rise above the need to impress others and begin to live life by your own rules. In 2012 consciousness, you will find that the "best of you" is still yet to come. You will begin to experience your own truth with the intuitive all-knowingness that is resonating within you. Your outside world will become less important, and you will feel calm and peaceful in all situations. You will understand the importance of having your own quiet time, and you'll want to clear your mind of all mental obstructions. Your inner-self will experience an expansion of Being, and your passions and creativity will find expression in the world. This part of you can no longer be denied and will flow out of your Being. *You will not be able to do otherwise.* You will find the courage, strength, and vitality to pursue your natural talents and bring out the beauty, goodness, and light that is your own special contribution to humanity.

In era-2012, you will have a choice to either participate in a cosmic regeneration of the Spirit or to hold onto the failed ideas of the past. You will know if you are moving in the right direction by simply asking yourself: "In my daily life, am I helping others or hurt-ing them?" When you answer this question honestly, you will know if your actions are contributing to the betterment of the world or holding it back. You always have the opportunity to change selfish-ness into self-*lessness* whenever and wherever you are. In 2012 con-sciousness, there are no regrets about the past or how you impeded your own progress. None of these self-degrading ideas will matter anymore. You will come to realize that you are the writer and direc-tor of your own daily script, and you can delete and add pages as you wish. You won't need to despair about perceived failures because you will come to realize that every experience has helped you along the way. It doesn't matter if the world has rejected your special gifts because you know more than the world.

You will be persistent in cultivating your talents and persevere whenever feeling rejected. You'll need to be patient and allow time for the world to catch up with you. Although you may have to wait for quite awhile, you will continue developing your inner gifts. You will find that your ability to learn has no beginning and no end, and just like the Mayan Calendar, you'll continue to begin a new, creative cycle.

The key to the Long Count Calendar is found when you apply it to yourself. It is the "Rosetta Stone" that will help you to decipher the meaning of your own life cycles. The five phases of the Calen-dar correspond to the five phases of your life. When you examine your life, you'll see that it can be broken down into five cycles of 20 years each, keeping in mind that 20 is the basis of the Mayan numerical system. Within each 20 year cycle you have changed your mind-set and your circumstances. Upon closer examination, each part of the twenty year cycle has four mini-cycles including a cre-ative, progressive, climatic, and regenerative phase. Right now, you are living in one of these phases, and you will continue experiencing different energies in each stage. Remember, only you can find the positive energies within a given cycle. Likewise, the same holds true for humanity's collective search to find positive energies as it moves through a mega-cycle.

The human phenomenon of collective consciousness is always progressing in a forward direction. Don't be frustrated when it seems as though nothing is changing. You can rest assured that humanity is slowly shifting to a higher plane of thought, and the beginning of the next cycle is now in view. This is a great time to be alive, and you are fortunate to participate in the continuation of the Long Count Cycle. Contrary to what people say, the world situation is *not* out of control, and those who propound such negative sentiments are *not helping the planet, themselves, or anyone else.* Fortunately, the goodness of the collective consciousness is always the greatest force in the Universe, and no one should ever underestimate the power of the *good* in people.

As each moment passes, you are getting closer to the life you have envisioned for yourself. The part of you that is filled with imagination and creativity is slowly being released into the world. When you know what you want in life, you'll see many opportunities right in front of you. There are always clues around you, but you need to pay attention to them. By observing the world in this manner, you will see a natural path appearing before you—and your "inner calendar" will always tell you when the time is approaching for necessary change. When this shift occurs, you will start seeing results immediately. You'll also see a perfect assimilation of your inner and outer worlds, and feelings of unity will fill the core of your Being.

The essence of these messages is found within the Mayan culture. Their intentions are noble, and they envision an optimistic future with a bright light shining on 2012. In the macrocosmic sense, the Mayans believed that the Universe is filled with love and natural beauty. In a microcosmic sense, they believed that each person is made of these same qualities.

Over the next few years, you and the majority of humanity will feel the irresistible power of 2012 consciousness tugging at you. As you participate in the emerging Age of the Fifth Sun, you will become part of a new inter-spiritual era as foreseen by the Mayan Elders.

2012: THE ULTIMATE MEANING

As we move toward 2012, a massive spiritual awakening will cause humanity to remember its inherent oneness. Although there are doubters, skeptics, and doomsayers who dismiss this idea, there are many more spiritual optimists who feel, understand, and just "know" that verifiable positive changes are taking place throughout the world. As for the arrival of December 21, 2012, it is becoming clear that humanity will be moving through a crucial time of progressive transformation.

As 2012 approaches, we are collectively in a transition phase of an Old World dying and a New World being born. According to the ancient Mayan Elders, the polarities and imbalances within us are changing and healing. Love, beauty, exuberance, and compassion are blossoming within young people, and universal spirituality, co-creation, community support, and healing are illuminating the spirited character of our true nature.

According to the Mayas, now is the time to embrace all that has been dishonored or denied. It is a time of purification and new beginnings as humanity moves forward into the next Golden Age. The cosmic climate is changing at a rapid pace, which allows us to transcend negative feelings of fear and limitation.

Significantly, the time has never been better for understanding that life is connected to one web of planetary singularity. Our challenge is to look within ourselves and establish balance and equilibrium within the seven levels of consciousness that are the building blocks of our total Being:

1. the physical body,

2. energy behind the breath of life,

3. the electrical body,

4. desires of the personality,

5. opening of the higher mind,

6. intuitive wisdom revealing itself, and

7. spiritual essence connecting to the Source.

These seven levels of consciousness need to be in alignment, so each individual can express his or her individuality and participate in the functioning of the whole. As frequencies continue to rise, our connection to other dimensions will increase rapidly. Accordingly, we will be swept up in a wave of maximum transformation which will determine who we will be and how life will unfold for us.

With doors of opportunity opening over the next few years, we will have no limitations other than those that are self-imposed. This is the moment to turn the dream of a united humanity into a future reality. Therefore, the meaning of 2012 reveals a hopeful message.

During the next Mayan Age of 5,125 years, all nationalities, cultures, races, and religions will continue blending together into One, Single, Unified Whole. This amalgamation of the human spirit will bring humanity one step closer to collectively experiencing the supernal nature of the Ultimate Reality. The days of prejudice, racism, cultural judgments, and bigotry will continue decreasing with each passing generation and will fade away in time. As we move closer to 2012 and beyond, our generation is about to witness the most awe-inspiring transition ever experienced by humanity—a giant leap in collective consciousness that is accelerating toward its future goal of becoming One with the All.